The

I0160834

REAL

Change

You can count on

Ron Berger

Published by:
berger publishing
Rancho Belago, CA 92555
mail@ronberger.com
http://www.ronberger.com

Printed in the USA
ISBN 13 - 978-0-9799257-7-1
ISBN 10 - 0-9799257-7-0
First Printing

Library of Congress Control Number
2010917472

Ron's Other Books

The House That Ron Built

Are You Being Served Yet?

P-NUT, The Love of a Dog

"Normal" MAYDAY

Time for TEA

Growing Old is a FULL-TIME JOB

Time for MORE TEA

Time for STILL MORE TEA

One Candle at a Time

LOOking @ ... Things in General

Contents

Before we start . . .

You really need to know that I am not a freak of nature or a racist or a spoiled sport or rabble rouser or even a doomsayer, but a true American Patriot that only wants the best for each citizen.

I have worked hard for what we have and I know that you have also and the thought of someone or something taking that away from me is very disturbing.

The mid-term elections of 2010 are now behind us and we are looking forward to another record busting election in 2012. Believe it or not - within a week of the Republicans taking back control of the House, they are indicating that they are now first among equals at the money trough.

However, the forthcoming election is just not between the Republicans and Democrats, but rather between Conservative and Liberal. Both political parties have fallen into the same trap and only tell you a different story just to get your vote. Both are politicians and that only means that corruption is close at hand.

We as citizens have to change how these politicians think and then hold their feet to the fire to get the job done. Politicians, on both sides of the isle have the same faults. We want our share of the "booty". They haven't learned yet that the well is so low that the hook they are fishing with isn't even getting wet. They were elected to figure out how to fill it up - not drain it more.

I've tried to deal with the mysterious in this book. What we see on the surface and what we are told are but a piece of the puzzle that is unfolding before our very own diminished vision.

I'm sure that many voters, as of the day after election 2010, feel that the conservatives are now in control of the money and things will get better real soon. There are various levels of understanding that most people don't understand.

First, you look at your own well-being. Then you look at your city's well-being, then your states and finally your country's. This is about as far as you can comprehend. But, there are further levels that we are very oblivious about. This is the level that I'm trying to explore. Republicans or Democrats come from the same mold, for the most part. Then why do we make such a fuss about who wins?

Don't get me wrong. There are still good people who want to solve this problem. We must continue to vote for the best and then closely monitor their every move. Once you understand the magnitude of the problem, you will want to find out much more. The internet is full of information that needs to be digested and acted upon.

If you are one that really doesn't care or are sucking up the milk from the fountain of money, this book may not make much sense to you. However, you need to read it so soon - I'll be able to tell you - "I told you so"!

I don't plan on being around too much longer and the problems we are facing now have less and less to do with me, but, my children and their children will soon realize that there was a _change_ and my generation had the ability to do something about it. They will no longer have the freedoms I had because the State has deemed it better that they live under the government's "protection".

This just isn't "our" government doing this protecting, but a New World Order designed to eliminate the middle class, reduce the population and make everyone subservient to it. Sound impossible? Believe me, it's happening at this very moment.

How do we change this? Maybe it's already too late. If not, electing those that understand and want to change this defeatist program and get back to what our fore-fathers planned for us. Ladies & Gentlemen, Boys & Girls of all ages, this New World Order is truly happening as we speak. We have, as President today, one of the most vocal and energetic leaders of this movement. Listen, read and respond to the terrible state of affairs that await us.

When we hear the words - "change" - most will automatically think that it means change for the "better". There are two meanings to change and the "other" one is what this book is about.

I have utilized many articles from the internet that I feel truly tell the state of the country. I apologize to anyone who's article I have used without permission. I feel that all the articles have helped us understand the complexities under which we live. I feel it is our combined duty to get the word out and alert the populous of these dangers so that they may take some action. Our country is under strange powers that most of us are not aware of and just leaving this information on the internet doesn't help.

The goal of this book is to place much of this important information in one place so that no one has to search the internet to find it. Google was a great help in developing this book.

My desire is that your curiosity will be aroused and you will dig for further information. There are literally hundreds and hundreds of sites to be explored and not all of them can be considered theories.

I also have doubts on some sites, but knowing what I do now, I have fewer doubts everyday.

May God have mercy on us.

Ron

After decades of broken politics in Washington, eight years of failed policies from George Bush, and twenty-one months of a campaign that has taken us from the rocky coast of Maine to the sunshine of California, we are one week away from change in America.

In one week, you can turn the page on policies that have put the greed and irresponsibility of Wall Street before the hard work and sacrifice of folks on Main Street.

In one week, you can choose policies that invest in our middle-class, create new jobs, and grow this economy from the bottom-up so that everyone has a chance to succeed; from the CEO to the secretary and the janitor; from the factory owner to the men and women who work on its floor.

In one week, you can put an end to the politics that would divide a nation just to win an election; that tries to pit region against region, city against town, Republican against Democrat; that asks us to fear at a time when we need hope.

In one week, at this defining moment in history, _you can give this country the change we need._

We began this journey in the depths of winter nearly two years ago, on the steps of the Old State Capitol in Springfield, Illinois. Back then, we didn't have much money or many endorsements. We weren't given much of a chance by the polls or the pundits, and we knew how steep our climb would be.

But I also knew this. I knew that the size of our challenges had outgrown the smallness of our politics. I believed that Democrats and Republicans and Americans of every political stripe were hungry for new ideas, new leadership, and a _new kind of politics_ one that favors common sense over ideology; one that focuses on those values and ideals we hold in common as Americans.

Most of all, I believed in your ability to make change happen. I knew that the American people were a decent, generous people who are willing to work hard and sacrifice for future generations. And I was convinced that when we come together, our voices are more powerful than the most entrenched lobbyists, or the most vicious political attacks, or the full force of a status quo in Washington that wants to keep things just the way they are.

Twenty-one months later, my faith in the American people has been vindicated. That's how we've come so far and so close because of you. _That's how we'll_ *change this country* with your help. And that's why we can't afford to slow down, sit back, or let up for one day, one minute, or one second in this last week. Not now. Not when so much is at stake.

We are in the middle of the worst economic crisis since the Great Depression. 760,000 workers have lost their jobs this year. Businesses and families can't get credit. Home values are falling. Pensions are disappearing. Wages are lower than they've been in a decade, at a time when the cost of health care and college have never been higher. It's getting harder and harder to make the mortgage, or fill up your gas tank, or even keep the electricity on at the end of the month.

At a moment like this, the last thing we can afford is four more years of the tired, old theory that says we should give more to billionaires and big corporations and hope that prosperity trickles down to everyone else. The last thing we can afford is four more years where no one in Washington is watching anyone on Wall Street because politicians and lobbyists killed common-sense regulations. Those are the theories that got us into this mess. They haven't worked, and it's time for change. That's why I'm running for President of the United States.

Now, Senator McCain has served this country honorably. And he can point to a few moments over the past eight years where he has broken from George Bush on torture, for example. He deserves credit for that. But when it comes to the economy when it comes to the central issue of this election the plain truth is that John McCain has stood with this President every step of the way. Voting for the Bush tax cuts for the wealthy that he once opposed. Voting for the Bush budgets that spent us into debt. Calling for less regulation twenty-one times just this year. Those are the facts.

And now, after twenty-one months and three debates, Senator McCain still has not been able to tell the American people a single major thing he'd do differently from George Bush when it comes to the economy. Senator McCain says that we can't spend the next four years waiting for our luck to change, but you understand that the biggest gamble we can take is embracing the same old Bush-McCain policies that have failed us for the last eight years.

It's not change when John McCain wants to give a $700,000 tax cut to the average Fortune 500 CEO. It's not change when he wants to give $200 billion to the biggest corporations or $4 billion to the oil companies or $300 billion to the same Wall Street banks that got us into this mess. It's not change when he comes up with a tax plan that doesn't give a penny of relief to more than 100 million middle-class Americans. That's not change.

Look we've tried it John McCain's way. We've tried it George Bush's way.

Deep down, Senator McCain knows that, which is why his campaign said that "if we keep talking about the economy, we're going to lose." That's why he's spending these last weeks calling me every name in the book.

Because that's how you play the game in Washington. If you can't beat your opponent's ideas, you distort those ideas and maybe make some up. If you don't have a record to run on, then you paint your opponent as someone people should run away from. You make a big election about small things.

Ohio, we are here to say "Not this time. Not this year. Not when so much is at stake." Senator McCain might be worried about losing an election, *but I'm worried about Americans who are losing their homes, and their jobs, and their life savings.* I can take one more week of John McCain's attacks, but this country can't take four more years of the same old politics and the same failed policies. It's time for something new.

The question in this election is not "Are you better off than you were four years ago?" We know the answer to that. *The real question is, "Will this country be better off four years from now?"*

I know these are difficult times for America. But I also know that we have faced difficult times before. The American story has never been about things coming easy it's been about rising to the moment when the moment was hard. It's about seeing the highest mountaintop from the deepest of valleys. It's about rejecting fear and division for unity of purpose. That's how we've overcome war and depression. That's how we've won great struggles for civil rights and women's rights and worker's rights. And that's how we'll emerge from this crisis stronger and more prosperous than we were before as one nation; as one people.

Remember, we still have the most talented, most productive workers of any country on Earth. We're still home to innovation and technology, colleges and universities that are the envy of the world. Some of the biggest ideas in history have come from our small businesses and our research facilities. So there's no reason we can't make this century another American century. We just need a new direction. We need a new politics.

Now, I don't believe that government can or should try to solve all our problems. I know you don't either. But I do believe that government should do that which we cannot do for ourselves   protect us from harm and provide a decent education for our children; invest in new roads and new science and technology. It should reward drive and innovation and growth in the free market, but it should also make sure businesses live up to their responsibility to create American jobs, and look out for American workers, and play by the rules of the road. It should ensure a shot at success not only for those with money and power and influence, but for every single American who's willing to work. That's how we create not just more millionaires, but more middle-class families. That's how we make sure businesses have customers that can afford their products and services.

That's how we've always grown the American economy   from the bottom-up. John McCain calls this socialism. I call it opportunity, and there is nothing more American than that.

Understand, if we want get through this crisis, we need to get beyond the old ideological debates and divides between left and right. _We don't need bigger government or smaller government. We need a better government   a more competent government   a government that upholds the values we hold in common as Americans._

We don't have to choose between allowing our financial system to collapse and spending billions of taxpayer dollars to bail out Wall Street banks. As President, I will ensure that the financial rescue plan helps stop foreclosures and protects your money instead of enriching CEOs. And I will put in place the common-sense regulations I've been calling for throughout this campaign so that Wall Street can never cause a crisis like this again. That's the change we need.

The choice in this election isn't between tax cuts and no tax cuts. It's about whether you believe we should only reward wealth, or whether we should also reward the work and workers who create it. I will give a tax break to 95% of Americans who work every day and get taxes taken out of their paychecks every week. I'll eliminate income taxes for seniors making under $50,000 and give homeowners and working parents more of a break. And I'll help pay for this by asking the folks who are making more than $250,000 a year to go back to the tax rate they were paying in the 1990s. No matter what Senator McCain may claim, *here are the facts if you make under $250,000, you will not see your taxes increase by a single dime not your income taxes, not your payroll taxes, not your capital gains taxes. Nothing. Because the last thing we should do in this economy is raise taxes on the middle-class.*

When it comes to jobs, the choice in this election is not between putting up a wall around America or allowing every job to disappear overseas. The truth is, we won't be able to bring back every job that we've lost, but that doesn't mean we should follow John

McCain's plan to keep giving tax breaks to corporations that send American jobs overseas. I will end those breaks as President, and I will give American businesses a $3,000 tax credit for every job they create right here in the United States of America. I'll eliminate capital gains taxes for small businesses and start-up companies that are the engine of job creation in this country. We'll create two million new jobs by rebuilding our crumbling roads, and bridges, and schools, and by laying broadband lines to reach every corner of the country. And I will invest $15 billion a year in renewable sources of energy to create five million new energy jobs over the next decade   jobs that pay well and can't be outsourced; jobs building solar panels and wind turbines and a new electricity grid; jobs building the fuel-efficient cars of tomorrow, not in Japan or South Korea but here in the United States of America; jobs that will help us eliminate the oil we import from the Middle East in ten years and help save the planet in the bargain. That's how America can lead again.

When it comes to health care, we don't have to choose between a government-run health care system and the unaffordable one we have now. *If you already have health insurance, the only thing that will change under my plan is that we will lower premiums.* If you don't have health insurance, *you'll be able to get the same kind of health insurance that Members of Congress get for themselves.* We'll invest in preventative care and new technology to finally lower the cost of health care for families, businesses, and the entire economy. And as someone who watched his own mother spend the final months of her life arguing with insurance companies because they claimed her cancer was a pre-existing condition and didn't want to pay for treatment, I will stop insurance companies from discriminating against those who are sick and need care most.

When it comes to giving every child a world-class education so they can compete in this global economy for the jobs of the 21st century, the choice is not between more money and more reform because our schools need both. As President, I will invest in early childhood education, recruit an army of new teachers, pay them more, and give them more support. But I will also demand higher standards and more accountability from our teachers and our schools. And I will make a deal with every American who has the drive and the will but not the money to go to college: *if you commit to serving your community or your country, we will make sure you can afford your tuition.* You invest in America, America will invest in you, and together, we will move this country forward.

And when it comes to keeping this country safe, we don't have to choose between retreating from the world and fighting a war without end in Iraq.

It's time to stop spending $10 billion a month in Iraq while the Iraqi government sits on a huge surplus. As President, I will end this war by asking the Iraqi government to step up, and finally finish the fight against bin Laden and the al Qaeda terrorists who attacked us on 9/11. I will never hesitate to defend this nation, but I will only send our troops into harm's way with a clear mission and a sacred commitment to give them the equipment they need in battle and the care and benefits they deserve when they come home. I will build new partnerships to defeat the threats of the 21st century, and I will restore our moral standing, so that America is once again that last, best hope for all who are called to the cause of freedom, who long for lives of peace, and who yearn for a better future.

I won't stand here and pretend that any of this will be easy especially now. _The cost of this economic crisis, and the cost of the war in Iraq, means that Washington will have to tighten its belt and put off spending on things we can afford to do without._ On this, there is no other choice. As President, _I will go through the federal budget, line-by-line, ending programs that we don't need and making the ones we do need work better and cost less._

But as I've said from the day we began this journey all those months ago, the change we need isn't just about new programs and policies. It's about a new politics a politics that calls on our better angels instead of encouraging our worst instincts; one that reminds us of the obligations we have to ourselves and one another.

Part of the reason this economic crisis occurred is because we have been living through an era of profound irresponsibility. On Wall Street, easy money and an ethic of "what's good for me is good enough" blinded greedy executives to the danger in the decisions they were making. On Main Street, lenders tricked people into buying homes they couldn't afford.

Some folks knew they couldn't afford those houses and bought them anyway. In Washington, politicians spent money they didn't have and allowed lobbyists to set the agenda. They scored political points instead of solving our problems, and even after the greatest attack on American soil since Pearl Harbor, all we were asked to do by our President was to go out and shop.

That is why what we have lost in these last eight years cannot be measured by lost wages or bigger trade deficits alone. What has also been lost is the idea that in this American story, each of us has a role to play. Each of us has a responsibility to work hard and look after ourselves and our families, and each of us has a responsibility to our fellow citizens. That's what's been lost these last eight years our sense of common purpose; of higher purpose. And that's what we need to restore right now.

Yes, government must lead the way on energy independence, but each of us must do our part to make our homes and our businesses more efficient. Yes, we must provide more ladders to success for young men who fall into lives of crime and despair. But all of us must do our part as parents to turn off the television and read to our children and take responsibility for providing the love and guidance they need. Yes, we can argue and debate our positions passionately, but at this defining moment, all of us must summon the strength and grace to bridge our differences and unite in common effort black, white, Latino, Asian, Native American; Democrat and Republican, young and old, rich and poor, gay and straight, disabled or not.
In this election, we cannot afford the same political games and tactics that are being used to pit us against one another and make us afraid of one another. The stakes are too high to divide us by class and region and background; by who we are or what we believe.

Because despite what our opponents may claim, there are no real or fake parts of this country. There is no city or town that is more pro-America than anywhere else we are one nation, all of us proud, all of us patriots. There are patriots who supported this war in Iraq and patriots who opposed it; patriots who believe in Democratic policies and those who believe in Republican policies. The men and women who serve in our battlefields may be Democrats and Republicans and Independents, but they have fought together and bled together and some died together under the same proud flag. They have not served a Red America or a Blue America they have served the United States of America.

It won't be easy, Ohio. It won't be quick. But you and I know that it is time to come together and change this country. Some of you may be cynical and fed up with politics. A lot of you may be disappointed and even angry with your leaders. You have every right to be. But despite all of this, I ask of you what has been asked of Americans throughout our history.

I ask you to believe not just in my ability to bring about change, but in yours.

I know this change is possible. Because I have seen it over the last twenty-one months. Because in this campaign, I have had the privilege to witness what is best in America.

I've seen it in lines of voters that stretched around schools and churches; in the young people who cast their ballot for the first time, and those not so young folks who got involved again after a very long time. I've seen it in the workers who would rather cut back their hours than see their friends lose their jobs; in the neighbors who take a stranger in when the floodwaters rise; in the soldiers who re-enlist after losing a limb. I've seen it in the faces of the men and women I've met at countless rallies and town halls across the country, men and women who speak of their struggles but also of their hopes and dreams.

I still remember the email that a woman named Robyn sent me after I met her in Ft. Lauderdale. Sometime after our event, her son nearly went into cardiac arrest, and was diagnosed with a heart condition that could only be treated with a procedure that cost tens of thousands of dollars. Her insurance company refused to pay, and their family just didn't have that kind of money.

In her email, Robyn wrote, "I ask only this of you on the days where you feel so tired you can't think of uttering another word to the people, think of us. When those who oppose you have you down, reach deep and fight back harder."

Ohio, that's what hope is that thing inside us that insists, despite all evidence to the contrary, that something better is waiting around the bend; that insists there are better days ahead. If we're willing to work for it. If we're willing to shed our fears and our doubts. If we're willing to reach deep down inside ourselves when we're tired and come back fighting harder.

Hope! That's what kept some of our parents and grandparents going when times were tough. What led them to say, "Maybe I can't go to college, but if I save a little bit each week my child can; maybe I can't have my own business but if I work really hard my child can open one of her own." It's what led immigrants from distant lands to come to these shores against great odds and carve a new life for their families in America; what led those who couldn't vote to march and organize and stand for freedom; that led them to cry out, "It may look dark tonight, but if I hold on to hope, tomorrow will be brighter."

That's what this election is about. That is the choice we face right now.
Don't believe for a second this election is over. Don't think for a minute that power concedes. We have to work like our future depends on it in this last week, because it does.

In one week, we can choose an economy that rewards work and creates new jobs and fuels prosperity from the bottom-up.

In one week, we can choose to invest in health care for our families, and education for our kids, and renewable energy for our future.

In one week, we can choose hope over fear, unity over division, the promise of change over the power of the status quo.

In one week, we can come together as one nation, and one people, and once more choose our better history.

That's what's at stake. That's what we're fighting for. And if in this last week, you will knock on some doors for me, and make some calls for me, and talk to your neighbors, and convince your friends; if you will stand with me, and fight with me, and give me your vote, then I promise you this we will not just win Ohio, we will not just win this election, but together, _we will change this country and we will change the world._ Thank you, God bless you, and may God bless America.

Now isn't that a great campaign speech? It really makes you want to go to the poles right now.   I know a lot of young voters fell for it. Those that are new to politics and haven't experienced how deceitful a candidate can really be.

I put BO's (Barack Obama in case you didn't figure that out) speech at the beginning to set the tone of this whole book. I've taken the liberty to underline some of the phrases that could lead many astray.

I'm not just talking about what BO is doing to this country, compared to what he promised, but rather showing that this slow transformation to a new world order is picking up steam.

I'm sure all of you have heard of the New World Order. It's been some time since it has come up, but the events of the last two years point to its existence and that the real meaning is starting to surface again.

BO did not invent NWO, but he sure has caught on fast as to how it works and how to push it along at an incredible rate.   We need to give some background as to how this all came about and what it feeds on.

First lets truly describe what kind of government we have (or had).

An Important Distinction: Democracy versus Republic

It is important to keep in mind the difference between a Democracy and a Republic, as dissimilar forms of government. Understanding the difference is essential to comprehension of the fundamentals involved. It should be noted, in passing, that use of the word Democracy as meaning merely the popular type of government--that is, featuring genuinely free elections by the people periodically-- is not helpful in discussing, as here, the difference between alternative and dissimilar forms of a popular government: a Democracy versus a Republic. This double meaning of Democracy--a popular-type government in general, as well as a specific form of popular government--needs to be made clear in any discussion, or writing, regarding this subject, for the sake of sound understanding.

These two forms of government: Democracy and Republic, are not only dissimilar but antithetical, reflecting the sharp contrast between (a) The Majority Unlimited, in a Democracy, lacking any legal safeguard of the rights of The Individual and The Minority, and (b) The Majority Limited, in a Republic under a written Constitution safeguarding the rights of The Individual and The Minority; as we shall now see.

A Democracy

The chief characteristic and distinguishing feature of a Democracy is: Rule by Omnipotent Majority. In a Democracy, The Individual, and any group of Individuals composing any Minority, have no protection against the unlimited power of The Majority. It is a case of Majority-over-Man.

This is true whether it be a Direct Democracy, or a Representative Democracy. In the direct type, applicable only to a small number of people as in the little city-states of ancient Greece, or in a New England town-meeting, all of the electorate assemble to debate and decide all government questions, and all decisions are reached by a majority vote (of at least half-plus-one). Decisions of The Majority in a New England town-meeting are, of course, subject to the Constitutions of the State and of the United States which protect The Individual's rights; so, in this case, The Majority is not omnipotent and such a town-meeting is, therefore, not an example of a true Direct Democracy. Under a Representative Democracy like Britain's parliamentary form of government, the people elect representatives to the national legislature--the elective body there being the House of Commons--and it functions by a similar vote of at least half-plus-one in making all legislative decisions.

In both the Direct type and the Representative type of Democracy, The Majority's power is absolute and unlimited; its decisions are unappealable under the legal system established to give effect to this form of government. This opens the door to unlimited Tyranny-by-Majority. This was what The Framers of the United States Constitution meant in 1787, in debates in the Federal (framing) Convention, when they condemned the "excesses of democracy" and abuses under any Democracy of the unalienable rights of The Individual by The Majority. Examples were provided in the immediate post-1776 years by the legislatures of some of the States. In reaction against earlier royal tyranny, which had been exercised through oppressions by royal governors and judges of the new State governments, while the legislatures acted as if they were virtually omnipotent. There were no effective State Constitutions to limit the legislatures because most State governments were operating under mere Acts of their respective legislatures which were mislabeled "Constitutions." Neither the governors not the courts of the offending States were able to exercise any substantial and effective restraining influence upon the legislatures in defense of The Individual's unalienable rights, when violated by legislative infringements. (Connecticut and Rhode Island continued under their old Charters for many years.) It was not until 1780 that the first genuine Republic through constitutionally limited government, was adopted by Massachusetts--next New Hampshire in 1784, other States later.

It was in this connection that Jefferson, in his "Notes On The State of Virginia" written in 1781-1782, protected against such excesses by the Virginia Legislature in the years following the Declaration of Independence, saying: "An elective despotism was not the government we fought for . . ." (Emphasis Jefferson's.) He also denounced the despotic concentration of power in the Virginia Legislature, under the so-called "Constitution"--in reality a mere Act of that body:

"All the powers of government, legislative, executive, judiciary, result to the legislative body. The concentrating these in the same hands is precisely the definition of despotic government. It will be no alleviation that these powers will be exercised by a plurality of hands, and not by a single one. 173 despots would surely be as oppressive as one. Let those who doubt it turn their eyes on the republic of Venice."

This topic--the danger to the people's liberties due to the turbulence of democracies and omnipotent, legislative majority--is discussed in The Federalist, for example in numbers 10 and 48 by Madison (in the latter noting Jefferson's above-quoted comments).

The Framing Convention's records prove that by decrying the "excesses of democracy" The Framers were, of course, not opposing a popular type of government for the United States; their whole aim and effort was to create a sound system of this type. To contend to the contrary is to falsify history. Such a falsification not only maligns the high purpose and good character of The Framers but belittles the spirit of the truly Free Man in America-- the people at large of that period--who happily accepted and lived with gratification under the Constitution as their own fundamental law and under the Republic which it created, especially because they felt confident for the first time of the security of their liberties thereby protected against abuse by all possible violators, including The Majority momentarily in control of government. The truth is that The Framers, by their protests against the "excesses of democracy," were merely making clear their sound reasons for preferring a Republic as the proper form of government. They well knew, in light of history, that nothing but a Republic can provide the best safeguards--in truth in the long run the only effective safeguards (if enforced in practice)--for the people's liberties which are inescapably victimized by Democracy's form and system of unlimited Government-over-Man featuring The Majority Omnipotent. They also knew that the American people would not consent to any form of government but that of a Republic. It is of special interest to note that Jefferson, who had been in Paris as the American Minister for several years, wrote Madison from there in March 1789 that:

"The tyranny of the legislatures is the most formidable dread at present, and will be for long years. That of the executive will come it's turn, but it will be at a remote period." (Text per original.)

Somewhat earlier, Madison had written Jefferson about violation of the Bill of Rights by State legislatures, stating:

"Repeated violations of those parchment barriers have been committed by overbearing majorities in every State. In Virginia I have seen the bill of rights violated in every instance where it has been opposed to a popular current."

It is correct to say that in any Democracy--either a Direct or a Representative type--as a form of government, there can be no legal system which protects The Individual or The Minority (any or all minorities) against unlimited tyranny by The Majority. The undependable sense of self-restraint of the persons making up The Majority at any particular time offers, of course, no protection whatever. Such a form of government is characterized by The Majority Omnipotent and Unlimited. This is true, for example, of the Representative Democracy of Great Britain; because unlimited government power is possessed by the House of Lords, under an Act of Parliament of 1949--indeed, it has power to abolish anything and everything governmental in Great Britain.

For a period of some centuries ago, some English judges did argue that their decisions could restrain Parliament; but this theory had to be abandoned because it was found to be untenable in the light of sound political theory and governmental realities in a Representative Democracy. Under this form of government, neither the courts not any other part of the government can effectively challenge, much less block, any action by The Majority in the legislative body, no matter how arbitrary, tyrannous, or totalitarian they might become in practice. The parliamentary system of Great Britain is a perfect example of Representative Democracy and of the potential tyranny inherent in its system of Unlimited Rule by Omnipotent Majority. This pertains only to the potential, to the theory, involved; governmental practices there are irrelevant to this discussion.

Madison's observations in The Federalist number 10 are noteworthy at this point because they highlight a grave error made through the centuries regarding Democracy as a form of government. He commented as follows:
"Theoretic politicians, who have patronized this species of government, have erroneously supposed, that by reducing mankind to a perfect equality in their political rights, they would, at the same time, be perfectly equalized and assimilated in their possessions, their opinions, and their passions."

Democracy, as a form of government, is utterly repugnant to--is the very antithesis of--the traditional American system: that of a Republic, and its underlying philosophy, as expressed in essence in the Declaration of Independence with primary emphasis upon the people's forming their government so as to permit them to possess only "just powers" (limited powers) in order to make and keep secure the God-given, unalienable rights of each and every Individual and therefore of all groups of Individuals.

A Republic

A Republic, on the other hand, has a very different purpose and an entirely different form, or system, of government. Its purpose is to control The Majority strictly, as well as all others among the people, primarily to protect The Individual's God-given, unalienable rights and therefore for the protection of the rights of The Minority, of all minorities, and the liberties of people in general. The definition of a Republic is: a constitutionally limited government of the representative type, created by a written Constitution--adopted by the people and changeable (from its original meaning) by them only by its amendment--with its powers divided between three separate Branches: Executive, Legislative and Judicial. Here the term "the people" means, of course, the electorate.

The people adopt the Constitution as their fundamental law by utilizing a Constitutional Convention--especially chosen by them for this express and sole purpose--to frame it for consideration and approval by them either directly or by their representatives in a Ratifying Convention, similarly chosen. Such a Constitutional Convention, for either framing or ratification, is one of America's greatest contributions, if not her greatest contribution, to the mechanics of government--of self-government through constitutionally limited government, comparable in importance to America's greatest contribution to the science of government: the formation and adoption by the sovereign people of a written Constitution as the basis for self-government. One of the earliest, if not the first, specific discussions of this new American development (a Constitutional Convention) in the historical records is an entry in June 1775 in John Adams' "Autobiography" commenting on the framing by a convention and ratification by the people as follows:

"By conventions of representatives, freely, fairly, and proportionately chosen . . . the convention may send out their project of a constitution, to the people in their several towns, counties, or districts, and the people may make the acceptance of it their own act."

Yet the first proposal in 1778 of a Constitution for Massachusetts was rejected for the reason, in part, as stated in the "Essex Result" (the result, or report, of the Convention of towns of Essex County), that it had been framed and proposed not by a specially chosen convention but by members of the legislature who were involved in general legislative duties, including those pertaining to the conduct of the war.

The first genuine and soundly founded Republic in all history was the one created by the first genuine Constitution, which was adopted by the people of Massachusetts in 1780 after being framed for their consideration by a specially chosen Constitutional Convention. (As previously noted, the so-called "Constitutions" adopted by some States in 1776 were mere Acts of Legislatures, not genuine Constitutions.) That Constitutional Convention of Massachusetts was the first successful one ever held in the world; although New Hampshire had earlier held one unsuccessfully - it took several years and several successive conventions to produce the New Hampshire Constitution of 1784. Next, in 1787-1788, the United States Constitution was framed by the Federal Convention for the people's consideration and then ratified by the people of the several States through a Ratifying Convention in each State specially chosen by them for this sole purpose. Thereafter the other States gradually followed in general the Massachusetts pattern of Constitution-making in adoption of genuine Constitutions; but there was a delay of a number of years in this regard as to some of them, several decades as to a few.

This system of Constitution-making, for the purpose of establishing constitutionally limited government, is designed to put into practice the principle of the Declaration of Independence: that the people form their governments and grant to them only "just powers," limited powers, in order primarily to secure (to make and keep secure) their God-given, unalienable rights. The American philosophy and system of government thus bar equally the "snob-rule" of a governing Elite and the "mob-rule" of an Omnipotent Majority. This is designed, above all else, to preclude the existence in America of any governmental power capable of being misused so as to violate The Individual's rights--to endanger the people's liberties.

With regard to the republican form of government (that of a republic), Madison made an observation in The Federalist (no. 55) which merits quoting here--as follows:

"As there is a degree of depravity in mankind which requires a certain degree of circumspection and distrust: So there are other qualities in human nature, which justify a certain portion of esteem and confidence. Republican government (that of a Republic) presupposes the existence of these qualities in a higher degree than any other form. Were the pictures which have been drawn by the political jealousy of some among us, faithful likenesses of the human character, the inference would be that there is not sufficient virtue among men for self government; and that nothing less than the chains of despotism can restrain them from destroying and devouring one another." (Emphasis added.)

It is noteworthy here that the above discussion, though brief, is sufficient to indicate the reasons why the label "Republic" has been misapplied in other countries to other and different forms of government throughout history. It has been greatly misunderstood and widely misused--for example as long ago as the time of Plato, when he wrote his celebrated volume, The Republic; in which he did not discuss anything governmental even remotely resembling--having essential characteristics of--a genuine Republic. Frequent reference is to be found, in the writings of the period of the framing of the Constitution for instance, to "the ancient republics," but in any such connection the term was used loosely--by way of contrast to a monarchy or to a Direct Democracy--often using the term in the sense merely of a system of Rule-by-Law featuring Representative government; as indicated, for example, by John Adams in his "Thoughts on Government" and by Madison in The Federalist numbers 10 and 39. But this is an incomplete definition because it can include a Representative Democracy, lacking a written Constitution limiting The Majority.

From The American Ideal of 1776: The Twelve Basic American Principles.

I pledge allegiance to the flag
of the United States of America
and to the REPUBLIC for which it stands
one nation, under God,
with liberty and justice for all.

How many times have you made this pledge and didn't realize everything you were saying? Most of us only have heard the controversy in the saying of "under God" that we didn't realize that the framers of the constitution didn't set us up with a democracy type government, but rather a Republic.

Now the Democrats would like you to believe we have a democracy and not a republic. Thus their name - "Democrats". Now you will also note that the Republicans derived their name from the republic form of government we started out with.

This is not to say that one is right and the other wrong. Both parties can claim their share of corruption, lies, broken promises and uttered falsehoods. Both are not worthy to say they represent the citizens of the United States. Both are there to stay there - if they can help it - and it would take the uproar of the citizenry to get them out.

We now need to go back in time and find out how and when the NWO came about.

A CHRONOLOGICAL HISTORY OF THE NEW WORLD ORDER
by D.L. Cuddy, Ph.D.

Arranged and Edited by John Loeffler
In the mainline media, those who adhere to the position that there is some kind of "conspiracy" pushing us towards a world government are virulently ridiculed. The standard attack maintains that the so-called "New World Order" is the product of turn-of-the-century, right-wing, bigoted, anti-semitic racists acting in the tradition of the long-debunked Protocols of the Learned Elders of Zion, now promulgated by some Militias and other right-wing hate groups.

The historical record does not support that position to any large degree but it has become the mantra of the socialist left and their cronies, the media.

The term "New World Order" has been used thousands of times in this century by proponents in high places of federalized world government.

Some of those involved in this collaboration to achieve world order have been Jewish. The preponderance are not, so it most definitely is not a Jewish agenda.

For years, leaders in education, industry, the media, banking, etc., have promoted those with the same Weltanschauung (world view) as theirs. Of course, someone might say that just because individuals promote their friends doesn't constitute a conspiracy. That's true in the usual sense. However, it does represent an "open conspiracy," as described by noted Fabian Socialist H.G. Wells in The Open Conspiracy: Blue Prints for a World Revolution (1928).

In 1913, prior to the passage of the Federal Reserve Act President Wilson's The New Freedom was published, in which he revealed: "Since I entered politics, I have chiefly had men's views confided to me privately. Some of the biggest men in the U. S., in the field of commerce and manufacturing, are afraid of somebody, are afraid of something. They know that there is a power somewhere so organized, so subtle, so watchful, so interlocked, so complete, so pervasive, that they had better not speak above their breath when they speak in condemnation of it."

On November 21, 1933, President Franklin Roosevelt wrote a letter to Col. Edward Mandell House, President Woodrow Wilson's close advisor: "The real truth of the matter is, as you and I know, that a financial element in the larger centers has owned the Government ever since the days of Andrew Jackson... "

That there is such a thing as a cabal of power brokers who control government behind the scenes has been detailed several times in this century by credible sources. Professor Carroll Quigley was Bill Clinton's mentor at Georgetown University. President Clinton has publicly paid homage to the influence Professor Quigley had on his life.

In Quigley's magnum opus Tragedy and Hope (1966), he states: "There does exist and has existed for a generation, an international ... network which operates, to some extent, in the way the radical right believes the Communists act. In fact, this network, which we may identify as the Round Table Groups, has no aversion to cooperating with the Communists, or any other groups and frequently does so. I know of the operations of this network because I have studied it for twenty years and was permitted for two years, in the early 1960s, to examine its papers and secret records. I have no aversion to it or to most of its aims and have, for much of my life, been close to it and to many of its instruments. I have objected, both in the past and recently, to a few of its policies... but in general my chief difference of opinion is that it wishes to remain unknown, and I believe its role in history is significant enough to be known."

Even talk show host Rush Limbaugh, an outspoken critic of anyone claiming a push for global government, said on his February 7, 1995 program: "You see, if you amount to anything in Washington these days, it is because you have been plucked or handpicked from an Ivy League school -- Harvard,

Yale, Kennedy School of Government -- you've shown an aptitude to be a good Ivy League type, and so you're plucked so-to-speak, and you are assigned success. You are assigned a certain role in government somewhere, and then your success is monitored and tracked, and you go where the pluckers and the handpickers can put you."

On May 4, 1993, Council on Foreign Relations (CFR) president Leslie Gelb said on The Charlie Rose Show that: "... you [Charlie Rose] had me on [before] to talk about the New World Order! I talk about it all the time. It's one world now. The Council [CFR] can find, nurture, and begin to put people in the kinds of jobs this country needs. And that's going to be one of the major enterprises of the Council under me."

Previous CFR chairman, John J. McCloy (1953-70), actually said they have been doing this since the 1940s (and before). The thrust towards global government can be well-documented but at the end of the twentieth century it does not look like a traditional conspiracy in the usual sense of a secret cabal of evil men meeting clandestinely behind closed doors. Rather, it is a "networking" of like-minded individuals in high places to achieve a common goal, as described in Marilyn Ferguson's 1980 insider classic, The Aquarian Conspiracy.

Perhaps the best way to relate this would be a brief history of the New World Order, not in our words but in the words of those who have been striving to make it real.

1912 -- Colonel Edward M. House, a close advisor of President Woodrow Wilson, publishes Phillip Dru: Administrator in which he promotes "socialism as dreamed of by Karl Marx."

1913 -- The Federal Reserve (neither federal nor a reserve) is created. It was planned at a secret meeting in 1910 on Jekyl Island, Georgia by a group of bankers and politicians, including Col. House. This transferred the power to create money from the American government to a private group of bankers. It is probably the largest generator of debt in the world.

May 30, 1919 -- Prominent British and American personalities establish the Royal Institute of International Affairs in England and the Institute of International Affairs in the U.S. at a meeting arranged by Col. House attended by various Fabian socialists, including noted economist John Maynard Keynes. Two years later, Col. House reorganizes the Institute of International Affairs into the Council on Foreign Relations (CFR).

December 15, 1922 -- The CFR endorses World Government in its magazine Foreign Affairs. Author Philip Kerr, states: "Obviously there is going to be no peace or prosperity for mankind as long as [the earth] remains divided into 50 or 60 independent states until some kind of international system is created... The real problem today is that of the world government."

1928 -- The Open Conspiracy: Blue Prints for a World Revolution by H.G. Wells is published. A former Fabian Socialist, Wells writes: "The political world of the ... Open Conspiracy must weaken, efface, incorporate and supersede existing governments... The Open Conspiracy is the natural inheritor of socialist and communist enthusiasms; it may be in control of Moscow before it is in control of New York... The character of the Open Conspiracy will now be plainly displayed... It will be a world religion."

1931 -- Students at the Lenin School of Political Warfare in Moscow are taught: "One day we shall start to spread the most theatrical peace movement the world has ever seen. The capitalist countries, stupid and decadent ... will fall into the trap offered by the possibility of making new friends. Our day will come in 30 years or so... The bourgeoisie must be lulled into a false sense of security."

1931 -- In a speech to the Institute for the Study of International Affairs at Copenhagen) historian Arnold Toyee said: "We are at present working discreetly with all our might to wrest this mysterious force called sovereignty out of the clutches of the local nation states of the world. All the time we are denying with our lips what we are doing with our hands...."

1932 -- New books are published urging World Order: Toward Soviet America by William Z. Foster. Head of the Communist Party USA, Foster indicates that a National Department of Education would be one of the means used to develop a new socialist society in the U.S. The New World Order by F.S. Marvin, describing the League of Nations as the first attempt at a New World Order. Marvin says, "nationality must rank below the claims of mankind as a whole."

Dare the School Build a New Social Order? is published. Educator author George Counts asserts that:
"... the teachers should deliberately reach for power and then make the most of their conquest" in order to "influence the social attitudes, ideals and behavior of the coming generation... The growth of science and technology has carried us into a new age where ignorance must be replaced by knowledge, competition by cooperation, trust in Providence by careful planning and private capitalism by some form of social economy."
1933 -- The first Humanist Manifesto is published. Co-author John Dewey, the noted philosopher and educator, calls for a synthesizing of all religions and "a socialized and cooperative economic order."
Co-signer C.F. Potter said in 1930: "Education is thus a most powerful ally of humanism, and every American public school is a school of humanism. What can the theistic Sunday schools, meeting for

an hour once a week, teaching only a fraction of the children, do to stem the tide of a five-day program of humanistic teaching?"

1933 -- The Shape of Things to Come by H.G. Wells is published. Wells predicts a second world war around 1940, originating from a German-Polish dispute. After 1945 there would be an increasing lack of public safety in "criminally infected" areas. The plan for the "Modern World-State" would succeed on its third attempt (about 1980), and come out of something that occurred in Basra, Iraq. The book also states, "Although world government had been plainly coming for some years, although it had been endlessly feared and murmured against, it found no opposition prepared anywhere."

1934 -- The Externalization of the Hierarchy by Alice A. Bailey is published. Bailey is an occultist, whose works are channeled from a spirit guide, the Tibetan Master [demon spirit] Djwahl Kuhl. Bailey uses the phrase "points of light" in connection with a "New Group of World

Servers" and claims that 1934 marks the beginning of "the organizing of the men and women... group work of a new order... [with] progress defined by service... the world of the Brotherhood... the Forces of Light... [and] out of the spoliation of all existing culture and civilization, the new world order must be built."

The book is published by the Lucis Trust, incorporated originally in New York as the Lucifer Publishing Company. Lucis Trust is a United Nations NGO and has been a major player at the recent U.N. summits. Later Assistant Secretary General of the U.N. Robert Mueller would credit the creation of his World Core Curriculum for education to the underlying teachings of Djwahl Kuhl via Alice Bailey's writings on the subject.

1932 -- Plan for Peace by American Birth Control League founder Margaret Sanger (1921) is published. She calls for coercive sterilization, mandatory segregation, and rehabilitative concentration camps for all "dysgenic stocks" including Blacks, Hispanics, American Indians and Catholics.

October 28, 1939 -- In an address by John Foster Dulles, later U.S. Secretary of State, he proposes that America lead the transition to a new order of less independent, semi-sovereign states bound together by a league or federal union.

1939 -- New World Order by H. G. Wells proposes a collectivist one-world state"' or "new world order" comprised of "socialist democracies." He advocates "universal conscription for service" and declares that "nationalist individualism... is the world's disease." He continues: "The manifest necessity for some collective world control to eliminate warfare and the less generally admitted necessity for a collective control of the economic and biological life of mankind, are aspects of one and the same process." He proposes that this be accomplished through "universal law" and propaganda (or education)."

1940 -- The New World Order is published by the Carnegie Endowment for International Peace and contains a select list of references on regional and world federation, together with some special plans for world order after the war.

December 12, 1940 -- In The Congressional Record an article entitled A New World Order John G. Alexander calls for a world federation.

1942 -- The leftist Institute of Pacific Relations publishes Post War Worlds by P.E. Corbett: "World government is the ultimate aim... It must be recognized that the law of nations takes precedence over national law... The process will have to be assisted by the deletion of the nationalistic material employed in educational textbooks and its replacement by material explaining the benefits of wiser association."

June 28, 1945 -- President Truman endorses world government in a speech: "It will be just as easy for nations to get along in a republic of the world as it is for us to get along in a republic of the United States."

October 24, 1945 -- The United Nations Charter becomes effective. Also on October 24, Senator Glen Taylor (D-Idaho) introduces Senate Resolution 183 calling upon the U.S. Senate to go on record as favoring creation of a world republic including an international police force.

1946 -- Alger Hiss is elected President of the Carnegie Endowment for International Peace. Hiss holds this office until 1949. Early in 1950, he is convicted of perjury and sentenced to prison after a sensational trial and Congressional hearing in which Whittaker Chambers, a former senior editor of Time, testifies that Hiss was a member of his Communist Party cell.

1946 -- The Teacher and World Government by former editor of the NEA Journal (National Education Association) Joy Elmer Morgan is published. He says: "In the struggle to establish an adequate world government, the teacher... can do much to prepare the hearts and minds of children for global understanding and cooperation... At the very heart of all the agencies which will assure the coming of world government must stand the school, the teacher, and the organized profession."

1947 -- The American Education Fellowship, formerly the Progressive Education Association, organized by John Dewey, calls for the:"... establishment of a genuine world order, an order in which national sovereignty is subordinate to world authority... "

October, 1947 -- NEA Associate Secretary William Carr writes in the NEA Journal that teachers should: "... teach about the various proposals that have been made for the strengthening of the United Nations and the establishment of a world citizenship and world government."

1948 -- Walden II by behavioral psychologist B.F. Skinner proposes "a perfect society or new and more perfect order" in which children are reared by the State, rather than by their parents and are trained from birth to demonstrate only desirable behavior and characteristics.

Skinner's ideas would be widely implemented by educators in the 1960s, 70s, and 80s as Values Clarification and Outcome Based Education.

July, 1948 -- Britain's Sir Harold Butler, in the CFR's Foreign Affairs, sees "a New World Order" taking shape: "How far can the life of nations, which for centuries have thought of themselves as distinct and unique, be merged with the life of other nations? How far are they prepared to sacrifice a part of their sovereignty without which there can be no effective economic or political union?... Out of the prevailing confusion a new world is taking shape... which may point the way toward the new order... That will be the beginning of a real United

Nations, no longer crippled by a split personality, but held together by a common faith."

1948 -- UNESCO president and Fabian Socialist, Sir Julian Huxley, calls for a radical eugenic policy in UNESCO: Its Purpose and Its Philosophy. He states: "Thus, even though it is quite true that any radical eugenic policy of controlled human breeding will be for many years politically and psychologically impossible, it will be important for UNESCO to see that the eugenic problem is examined with the greatest care and that the public mind is informed of the issues at stake that much that is now unthinkable may at least become thinkable."

1948 -- The preliminary draft of a World Constitution is published by U.S. educators advocating regional federation on the way toward world federation or government with England incorporated into a European federation.

The Constitution provides for a "World Council" along with a "Chamber of Guardians" to enforce world law. Also included is a "Preamble" calling upon nations to surrender their arms to the world government, and includes the right of this "Federal Republic of the World" to seize private property for federal use.

February 9, 1950 -- The Senate Foreign Relations Subcommittee introduces Senate Concurrent

Resolution 66 which begins: "Whereas, in order to achieve universal peace and justice, the present Charter of the United Nations should be changed to provide a true world government constitution."

The resolution was first introduced in the Senate on September 13, 1949 by Senator Glen Taylor (D-Idaho). Senator Alexander Wiley (R-Wisconsin) called it "a consummation devoutly to be wished for" and said, "I understand your proposition is either change the United Nations, or change or create, by a separate convention, a world order." Senator Taylor later stated: "We would have to sacrifice considerable sovereignty to the world organization to enable them to levy taxes in their own right to support themselves."

1950 -- In testimony before the Senate Foreign Relations Committee, international financier James P Warburg said: "we shall have a world government, whether or not we like it. The question is only whether world government will be achieved by consent or by conquest."

April 12, 1952 -- John Foster Dulles, later to become Secretary of State, says in a speech to the American Bar Association in Louisville, Kentucky, that "treaty laws can override the Constitution." He says treaties can take power away from Congress and give them to the President. They can take powers from the States and give them to the Federal Government or to some international body and they can cut across the rights given to the people by their constitutional Bill of Rights. A Senate amendment, proposed by GOP Senator John Bricker, would have provided that no treaty could supersede the Constitution, but it fails to pass by one vote.

1954 -- Prince Bernhard of the Netherlands establishes the Bilderbergers, international politicians and bankers who meet secretly on an annual basis.

1954 -- H. Rowan Gaither, Jr., President - Ford Foundation said to Norman Dodd of the Congressional Reese Commission: "... all of us here at the policy-making level have had experience with directives... from the White House.... The substance of them is that we shall use our grant-making power so as to alter our life in the United States that we can be comfortably merged with the Soviet Union."

1954 -- Senator William Jenner said: "Today the path to total dictatorship in the United States can be laid by strictly legal means, unseen and unheard by the Congress, the President, or the people... outwardly we have a Constitutional government. We have operating within our government and political system, another body representing another form of government, a bureaucratic elite which believes our Constitution is outmoded and is sure that it is the winning side.... All the strange developments in the foreign policy agreements may be traced to this group who are going to make us over to suit their pleasure.... This political action group has its own local political support organizations, its own pressure groups, its own vested interests, its foothold within our government, and its own propaganda apparatus."

1958 -- World Peace through World Law is published, where authors Grenville Clark and Louis Sohn advocate using the U.N. as a governing body for the world, world disarmament, a world police force and legislature.

1959 -- The Council on Foreign Relations calls for a New International Order Study Number 7, issued on November 25, advocated: "... new international order [which] must be responsive to world aspirations for peace, for social and economic change... an international order... including states labeling themselves as 'socialist' [communist]."

1959 -- The World Constitution and Parliament Association is founded which later develops a Diagram of World Government under the Constitution for the Federation of Earth.

1959 -- The Mid-Century Challenge to U.S. Foreign Policy is published, sponsored by the Rockefeller Brothers' Fund. It explains that the U.S.: "... cannot escape, and indeed should welcome... the task which history has imposed on us. This is the task of helping to shape a new world order in all its dimensions -- spiritual, economic, political, social."

September 9, 1960 -- President Eisenhower signs Senate Joint Resolution 170, promoting the concept of a federal Atlantic Union. Pollster and Atlantic Union Committee treasurer, Elmo Roper, later delivers an address titled, The Goal Is Government of All the World, in which he states: "For it becomes clear that the first step toward World Government cannot be completed until we have advanced on the four fronts: the economic, the military, the political and the social."

1961 -- The U.S. State Department issues a plan to disarm all nations and arm the United Nations. State Department Document Number 7277 is entitled Freedom From War: The U.S. Program for General and Complete Disarmament in a Peaceful World. It details a three-stage plan to disarm all nations and arm the U.N. with the final stage in which "no state would have the military power to challenge the progressively strengthened U.N. Peace Force."

March 1, 1962 -- Sen. Clark speaking on the floor of the Senate about PL 87-297 which calls for the disbanding of all armed forces and the prohibition of their re-establishment in any form whatsoever. "... This program is the fixed, determined and approved policy of the government of the United States."

1962 -- New Calls for World Federalism. In a study titled, A World Effectively Controlled by the United Nations, CFR member Lincoln Bloomfield states: "... if the communist dynamic was greatly abated, the West might lose whatever incentive it has for world government."

The Future of Federalism by author Nelson Rockefeller is published. The one-time Governor of New York, claims that current events compellingly demand a "new world order," as the old order is crumbling, and there is "a new and free order struggling to be born." Rockefeller says there is: "a fever of nationalism... [but] the nation-state is becoming less and less competent to perform its international political tasks.... These are some of the reasons pressing us to lead vigorously toward the true building of a new world order... [with] voluntary service... and our dedicated faith in the brotherhood of all mankind.... Sooner perhaps than we may realize... there will evolve the bases for a federal structure of the free world."

1963 -- J. William Fulbright, Chairman of the Senate Foreign Relations Committee speaks at a symposium sponsored by the Fund for the Republic, a left-wing project of the Ford Foundation: "The case for government by elites is irrefutable... government by the people is possible but highly improbable."

1964 -- Taxonomy of Educational Objectives, Handbook II is published. Author Benjamin Bloom states: "... a large part of what we call 'good teaching' is the teacher's ability to attain affective objectives through challenging the students' fixed beliefs."

His Outcome-Based Education (OBE) method of teaching would first be tried as Mastery Learning in Chicago schools. After five years, Chicago students' test scores had plummeted causing outrage among parents. OBE would leave a trail of wreckage wherever it would be tried and under whatever name it would be used. At the same time, it would become crucial to globalists for overhauling the education system to promote attitude changes among school students.

1964 -- Visions of Order by Richard Weaver is published. He describes: "progressive educators as a 'revolutionary cabal' engaged in 'a systematic attempt to undermine society's traditions and beliefs.'"

1967 -- Richard Nixon calls for New World Order. In Asia after Vietnam, in the October issue of Foreign Affairs, Nixon writes of nations' dispositions to evolve regional approaches to development needs and to the evolution of a "new world order."

1968 -- Joy Elmer Morgan, former editor of the NEA Journal publishes The American Citizens

Handbook in which he says: "the coming of the United Nations and the urgent necessity that it evolve into a more comprehensive form of world government places upon the citizens of the United States an increased obligation to make the most of their citizenship which now widens into active world citizenship."

July 26, 1968 -- Nelson Rockefeller pledges support of the New World Order. In an Associated Press report, Rockefeller pledges that, "as President, he would work toward international creation of a new world order."

1970 -- Education and the mass media promote world order. In Thinking About A New World Order for the Decade 1990, author Ian Baldwin, Jr. asserts that: "... the World Law Fund has begun a worldwide research and educational program that will introduce a new, emerging discipline -- world order -- into educational curricula throughout the world... and to concentrate some of its energies on bringing basic world order concepts into the mass media again on a worldwide level."

1972 -- President Nixon visits China. In his toast to Chinese Premier Chou En-lai, former CFR member and now President, Richard Nixon, expresses "the hope that each of us has to build a new world order."

May 18, 1972 -- In speaking of the coming of world government, Roy M. Ash, director of the Office of Management and Budget, declares that: "within two decades the institutional framework for a world economic community will be in place... [and] aspects of individual sovereignty will be given over to a super-national authority."

1973 -- The Trilateral Commission is established. Banker David Rockefeller organizes this new private body and chooses Zbigniew Brzezinski, later National Security Advisor to President Carter, as the Commission's first director and invites Jimmy Carter to become a founding member.

1973 -- Humanist Manifesto II is published: "The next century can be and should be the humanistic century... we stand at the dawn of a new age... a secular society on a planetary scale.... As non-theists we begin with humans not God, nature not deity... we deplore the division of humankind on nationalistic grounds.... Thus we look to the development of a system of world law and a world order based upon transnational federal government.... The true revolution is occurring."

April, 1974 -- Former U. S. Deputy Assistant Secretary of State, Trilateralist and CFR member Richard Gardner's article The Hard Road to World Order is published in the CFR's Foreign Affairs where he states that: "the 'house of world order' will have to be built from the bottom up rather than from the top down... but an end run around national sovereignty, eroding it piece by piece, will accomplish much more than the old-fashioned frontal assault."

1974 -- The World Conference of Religion for Peace, held in Louvain, Belgium is held. Douglas Roche presents a report entitled We Can Achieve a New World Order.

The U.N. calls for wealth redistribution: In a report entitled New International Economic Order, the U.N. General Assembly outlines a plan to redistribute the wealth from the rich to the poor nations.

1975 -- A study titled, A New World Order, is published by the Center of International Studies, Woodrow Wilson School of Public and International Studies, Princeton University.

1975 -- In Congress, 32 Senators and 92 Representatives sign A Declaration of Interdependence, written by historian Henry Steele Commager. The Declaration states that: "we must join with others to bring forth a new world order... Narrow notions of national sovereignty must not be permitted to curtail that obligation."

Congresswoman Marjorie Holt refuses to sign the Declaration saying: "It calls for the surrender of our national sovereignty to international organizations. It declares that our economy should be regulated by international authorities. It proposes that we enter a 'new world order' that would redistribute the wealth created by the American people."

1975 -- Retired Navy Admiral Chester Ward, former Judge Advocate General of the U.S. Navy and former CFR member, writes in a critique that the goal of the CFR is the "submergence of U. S. sovereignty and national independence into an all powerful one-world government... "

1975 -- Kissinger on the Couch is published. Authors Phyllis Schlafly and former CFR member Chester Ward state: "Once the ruling members of the CFR have decided that the U.S. government should espouse a particular policy, the very substantial research facilities of the CFR are put to work to develop arguments, intellectual and emotional, to support the new policy and to confound, discredit, intellectually and politically, any opposition... "

1976 -- RIO: Reshaping the International Order is published by the globalist Club of Rome, calling for a new international order, including an economic redistribution of wealth.

1977 -- The Third Try at World Order is published. Author Harlan Cleveland of the Aspen Institute for Humanistic Studies calls for: "changing Americans' attitudes and institutions" for "complete disarmament (except for international soldiers)" and "for individual entitlement to food, health and education."

1977 -- Imperial Brain Trust by Laurence Shoup and William Minter is published. The book takes a critical look at the Council on Foreign Relations with chapters such as: Shaping a New World Order: The Council's Blueprint for Global Hegemony, 1939-1944 and Toward the 1980's: The Council's Plans for a New World Order.

1977 -- The Trilateral Connection appears in the July edition of Atlantic Monthly. Written by Jeremiah Novak, it says: "For the third time in this century, a group of American schools, businessmen, and government officials is planning to fashion a New World Order... "

1977 -- Leading educator Mortimer Adler publishes Philosopher at Large in which he says: "... if local civil government is necessary for local civil peace, then world civil government is necessary for world peace."

1979 -- Barry Goldwater, retiring Republican Senator from Arizona, publishes his autobiography With No Apologies. He writes: "In my view The Trilateral Commission represents a skillful, coordinated effort to seize control and consolidate the four centers of power -- political, monetary, intellectual, and ecclesiastical. All this is to be done in the interest of creating a more peaceful, more productive world community. What the Trilateralists truly intend is the creation of a worldwide economic power superior to the political governments of the nation-states involved. They believe the abundant materialism they propose to create will overwhelm existing differences. As managers and creators of the system they will rule the future."

1984 -- The Power to Lead is published. Author James McGregor Burns admits: "The framers of the U.S. constitution have simply been too shrewd for us. The have outwitted us. They designed separate institutions that cannot be unified by mechanical linkages, frail bridges, tinkering. If we are to 'turn the Founders upside down' -- we must directly confront the constitutional structure they erected."

1985 -- Norman Cousins, the honorary chairman of Planetary Citizens for the World We Chose, is quoted in Human Events: "World government is coming, in fact, it is inevitable. No arguments for or against it can change that fact."

Cousins was also president of the World Federalist Association, an affiliate of the World Association for World Federation (WAWF), headquartered in Amsterdam. WAWF is a leading force for world federal government and is accredited by the U.N. as a Non-Governmental Organization.

1987 -- The Secret Constitution and the Need for Constitutional Change is sponsored in part by the

Rockefeller Foundation. Some thoughts of author Arthur S. Miller are: "... a pervasive system of thought control exists in the United States... the citizenry is indoctrinated by employment of the mass media and the system of public education... people are told what to think about... the old order is crumbling... Nationalism should be seen as a dangerous social disease... A new vision is required to plan and manage the future, a global vision that will transcend national boundaries and eliminate the poison of nationalistic solutions... a new Constitution is necessary."

1988 -- Former Under-secretary of State and CFR member George Ball in a January 24 interview in the New York Times says: "The Cold War should no longer be the kind of obsessive concern that it is. Neither side is going to attack the other deliberately... If we could internationalize by using the U.N. in conjunction with the Soviet Union, because we now no longer have to fear, in most cases, a Soviet veto, then we could begin to transform the shape of the world and might get the U.N. back to doing something useful... Sooner or later we are going to have to face restructuring our institutions so that they are not confined merely to the nation-states. Start first on a regional and ultimately you could move to a world basis."

December 7, 1988 -- In an address to the U.N., Mikhail Gorbachev calls for mutual consensus: "World progress is only possible through a search for universal human consensus as we move forward to a new world order."

May 12, 1989 -- President Bush invites the Soviets to join World Order. Speaking to the graduating class at Texas A&M University, Mr. Bush states that the United States is ready to welcome the Soviet Union "back into the world order."

1989 -- Carl Bernstein's (Woodward and Bernstein of Watergate fame) book Loyalties: A Son's Memoir is published. His father and mother had been members of the Communist party. Bernstein's father tells his son about the book: "You're going to prove [Sen. Joseph] McCarthy was right, because all he was saying is that the system was loaded with Communists. And he was right... I'm worried about the kind of book you're going to write and about cleaning up McCarthy. The problem is that everybody said he was a liar; you're saying he was right... I agree that the Party was a force in the country."

1990 -- The World Federalist Association faults the American press. Writing in their Summer/Fall newsletter, Deputy Director Eric Cox describes world events over the past year or two and declares: "It's sad but true that the slow-witted American press has not grasped the significance of most of these developments. But most federalists know what is happening... And they are not frightened by the old bug-a-boo of sovereignty."

September 11, 1990 -- President Bush calls the Gulf War an opportunity for the New World Order. In an address to Congress entitled Toward a New World Order, Mr. Bush says: "The crisis in the Persian Gulf offers a rare opportunity to move toward an historic period of cooperation. Out of these troubled times... a new world order can emerge in which the nations of the world, east and west, north and south, can prosper and live in harmony.... Today the new world is struggling to be born."

September 25, 1990 -- In an address to the U.N., Soviet Foreign Minister Eduard Shevardnadze describes Iraq's invasion of Kuwait as "an act of terrorism [that] has been perpetrated against the emerging New World Order."

On December 31, Gorbachev declares that the New World Order would be ushered in by the Gulf Crisis.

October 1, 1990 -- In a U.N. address, President Bush speaks of the: "... collective strength of the world community expressed by the U.N. ... an historic movement towards a new world order... a new partnership of nations... a time when humankind came into its own... to bring about a revolution of the spirit and the mind and begin a journey into a... new age."

1991 -- Author Linda MacRae-Campbell publishes How to Start a Revolution at Your School in the publication In Context. She promotes the use of "change agents" as "self-acknowledged revolutionaries" and "co-conspirators."

1991 -- President Bush praises the New World Order in a State of Union Message: "What is at stake is more than one small country, it is a big idea -- a new world order... to achieve the universal aspirations of mankind... based on shared principles and the rule of law.... The illumination of a thousand points of light.... The winds of change are with us now."

February 6, 1991 -- President Bush tells the Economic Club of New York: "My vision of a new world order foresees a United Nations with a revitalized peacekeeping function."

June, 1991 -- The Council on Foreign Relations co-sponsors an assembly Rethinking America's Security: Beyond Cold War to New World Order which is attended by 65 prestigious members of government, labor, academia, the media, military, and the professions from nine countries. Later, several of the conference participants joined some 100 other world leaders for another closed door meeting of the Bilderberg Society in Baden Baden, Germany. The Bilderbergers also exert considerable clout in determining the foreign policies of their respective governments. While at that meeting, David Rockefeller said in a speech: "We are grateful to the Washington Post, The New York Times, Time Magazine and other great publications whose directors have attended our meetings and respected their promises of discretion for almost forty years. It would have been impossible for us to develop our plan for the world if we had been subjected to the lights of publicity during those years. But, the world is now more sophisticated and prepared to march towards a world government. The supranational sovereignty of an intellectual elite and world bankers is surely preferable to the national auto-determination practiced in past centuries."

July, 1991 -- The Southeastern World Affairs Institute discusses the New World Order. In a program, topics include, Legal Structures for a New World Order and The United Nations: From its Conception to a New World Order. Participants include a former director of the U.N.'s General Legal Division, and a former Secretary General of International Planned Parenthood.

Late July, 1991 -- On a Cable News Network program, CFR member and former CIA director Stansfield Turner (Rhodes scholar), when asked about Iraq, responded: "We have a much bigger objective. We've got to look at the long run here. This is an example -- the situation between the United Nations and Iraq -- where the United Nations is deliberately intruding into the sovereignty of a sovereign nation... Now this is a marvelous precedent (to be used in) all countries of the world... "

October 29, 1991 -- David Funderburk, former U. S. Ambassador to Romania, tells a North Carolina audience: "George Bush has been surrounding himself with people who believe in one-world government. They believe that the Soviet system and the American system are converging." The vehicle to bring this about, said Funderburk, is the United Nations, "the majority of whose 166 member states are socialist, atheist, and anti-American." Funderburk served as ambassador in Bucharest from 1981 to 1985, when he resigned in frustration over U.S. support of the oppressive regime of the late Rumanian dictator, Nicolae Ceausescu.

October 30, 1991: -- President Gorbachev at the Middle East Peace Talks in Madrid states: "We are beginning to see practical support. And this is a very significant sign of the movement towards a new era, a new age... We see both in our country and elsewhere... ghosts of the old thinking... When we rid ourselves of their presence, we will be better able to move toward a new world order... relying on the relevant mechanisms of the United Nations."

Elsewhere, in Alexandria, Virginia, Elena Lenskaya, Counsellor to the Minister of Education of Russia, delivers the keynote address for a program titled, Education for a New World Order.

1992 -- The Twilight of Sovereignty by CFR member (and former Citicorp Chairman) Walter Wriston is published, in which he claims: "A truly global economy will require ... compromises of national sovereignty... There is no escaping the system."

1992 -- The United Nations Conference on Environment and Development (UNCED) Earth Summit takes place in Rio de Janeiro this year, headed by Conference Secretary-General Maurice Strong. The main products of this summit are the Biodiversity Treaty and Agenda 21, which the U.S. hesitates to sign because of opposition at home due to the threat to sovereignty and economics. The summit says the first world's wealth must be transferred to the third world.

July 20, 1992 -- Time magazine publishes The Birth of the Global Nation by Strobe Talbott, Rhodes Scholar, roommate of Bill Clinton at Oxford University, CFR Director, and Trilateralist, in which he writes: "All countries are basically social arrangements... No matter how permanent or even sacred they may seem at any one time, in fact they are all artificial and temporary... Perhaps national sovereignty wasn't such a great idea after all... But it has taken the events in our own wondrous and terrible century to clinch the case for world government."

As an editor of Time, Talbott defended Clinton during his presidential campaign. He was appointed by President Clinton as the number two person at the State Department behind Secretary of State Warren Christopher, former Trilateralist and former CFR Vice-Chairman and Director. Talbott was confirmed by about two-thirds of the U.S. Senate despite his statement about the unimportance of national sovereignty.

September 29, 1992 -- At a town hall meeting in Los Angeles, Trilateralist and former CFR president Winston Lord delivers a speech titled Changing Our Ways: America and the New World, in which he remarks: "To a certain extent, we are going to have to yield some of our sovereignty, which will be controversial at home... [Under] the North American Free Trade Agreement (NAFTA)... some Americans are going to be hurt as low-wage jobs are taken away." Lord became an Assistant Secretary of State in the Clinton administration.

1992 -- President Bush addressing the General Assembly of the U.N said: "It is the sacred principles enshrined in the United Nations charter to which the American people will henceforth pledge their allegiance."

Winter, 1992-93 -- The CFR's Foreign Affairs publishes Empowering the United Nations by U.N. Secretary General Boutros-Boutros Ghali, who asserts: "It is undeniable that the centuries-old doctrine of absolute and exclusive sovereignty no longer stands... Underlying the rights of the individual and the rights of peoples is a dimension of universal sovereignty that resides in all humanity... It is a sense that increasingly finds expression in the gradual expansion of international law... In this setting the significance of the United Nations should be evident and accepted."

1993 -- Strobe Talbott receives the Norman Cousins Global Governance Award for his 1992 Time article, The Birth of the Global Nation and in appreciation for what he has done "for the cause of global governance." President Clinton writes a letter of congratulation which states: "Norman Cousins worked for world peace and world government.... Strobe Talbott's lifetime achievements as a voice for global harmony have earned him this recognition... He will be a worthy recipient of the Norman Cousins Global Governance Award. Best wishes... for future success."

Not only does President Clinton use the specific term, "world government," but he also expressly wishes the WFA "future success" in pursuing world federal government. Talbott proudly accepts the award, but says the WFA should have given it to the other nominee, Mikhail Gorbachev.

July 18, 1993 -- CFR member and Trilateralist Henry Kissinger writes in the Los Angeles Times concerning NAFTA: "What Congress will have before it is not a conventional trade agreement but the architecture of a new international system... a first step toward a new world order."

August 23, 1993 -- Christopher Hitchens, Socialist friend of Bill Clinton when he was at Oxford University, says in a C-SPAN interview: "... it is, of course the case that there is a ruling class in this country, and that it has allies internationally."

October 30, 1993 -- Washington Post ombudsman Richard Harwood does an op-ed piece about the role of the CFR's media members: "Their membership is an acknowledgment of their ascension into the American ruling class [where] they do not merely analyze and interpret foreign policy for the United States; they help make it."

January/February, 1994 -- The CFR's Foreign Affairs prints an opening article by CFR Senior Fellow Michael Clough in which he writes that the "Wise Men" (e.g. Paul Nitze, Dean Acheson, George Kennan, and John J. McCloy) have: "assiduously guarded it [American foreign policy] for the past 50 years... They ascended to power during World War II... This was as it should be. National security and the national interest, they argued must transcend the special interests and passions of the people who make up America... How was this small band of Atlantic-minded internationalists able to triumph ... Eastern internationalists were able to shape and staff the burgeoning foreign policy institutions... As long as the Cold War endured and nuclear Armageddon seemed only a missile away, the public was willing to tolerate such an undemocratic foreign policy making system."

1994 -- In the Human Development Report, published by the UN Development Program, there was a section called "Global Governance For the 21st Century". The administrator for this program was appointed by Bill Clinton. His name is James Gustave Speth. The opening sentence of the report said: "Mankind's problems can no longer be solved by national government. What is needed is a World Government. This can best be achieved by strengthening the United Nations system."

1995 -- The State of the World Forum took place in the fall of this year, sponsored by the Gorbachev Foundation located at the Presidio in San Francisco. Foundation President Jim Garrison chairs the meeting of who's-whos from around the world including Margaret Thatcher, Maurice Strong, George Bush, Mikhail Gorbachev and others. Conversation centers around the oneness of mankind and the coming global government. However, the term "global governance" is now used in place of "new world order" since the latter has become a political liability, being a lightning rod for opponents of global government.

1996 -- The United Nations 420-page report Our Global Neighborhood is published. It outlines a plan for "global governance," calling for an international Conference on Global Governance in 1998 for the purpose of submitting to the world the necessary treaties and agreements for ratification by the year 2000.

There is a worldwide conspiracy being orchestrated by an extremely powerful and influential group of genetically-related individuals (at least at the highest echelons) which include many of the world's wealthiest people, top political leaders, and corporate elite, as well as members of the so-called Black Nobility of Europe (dominated by the British Crown) whose goal is to create a One World (fascist) Government, stripped of nationalistic and regional boundaries, that is obedient to their agenda. Their intention is to effect complete and total control over every human being on the planet and to dramatically reduce the world's population by 5.5 Billion people. While the name New World Order is a term frequently used today when referring to this group, it's more useful to identify the principal organizations, institutions, and individuals who make up this vast interlocking spiderweb of elite conspirators.

The Illuminati is the oldest term commonly used to refer to the 13 bloodline families (and their offshoots) that make up a major portion of this controlling elite. Most members of the Illuminati are also members in the highest ranks of numerous secretive and occult societies which in many cases extend straight back into the ancient world. The upper levels of the tightly compartmentalized (need-to-know-basis) Illuminati structural pyramid include planning committees and organizations that the public has little or no knowledge of. The upper levels of the Illuminati pyramid include secretive committees with names such as: the Council of 3, the Council of 5, the Council of 7, the Council of 9, the Council of 13, the Council of 33, the Grand Druid Council, the Committee of 300 (also called the "Olympians") and the Committee of 500 among others.

In 1992, Dr John Coleman published Conspirators' Hierarchy: The Story of the Committee of 300. With laudable scholarship and meticulous research, Dr Coleman identifies the players and carefully details the Illuminati agenda of worldwide domination and control. On page 161 of the Conspirators Hierarchy, Dr Coleman accurately summarizes the intent and purpose of the Committee of 300 as follows:

"A One World Government and one-unit monetary system, under permanent non-elected hereditary oligarchists who self-select from among their numbers in the form of a feudal system as it was in the Middle Ages. In this One World entity, population will be limited by restrictions on the number of children per family, diseases, wars, famines, until 1 billion people who are useful to the ruling class, in areas which will be strictly and clearly defined, remain as the total world population.

There will be no middle class, only rulers and the servants. All laws will be uniform under a legal system of world courts practicing the same unified code of   laws, backed up by a One World Government police force and a One World unified military to enforce laws in all former countries where no national boundaries shall exist. The system will be on the basis of a welfare state; those who are obedient and subservient to the One World Government will be rewarded with the means to live; those who are rebellious will simple be starved to death or be declared outlaws, thus a target for anyone who wishes to kill them. Privately owned firearms or weapons of any kind will be prohibited."

The sheer magnitude and complex web of deceit surrounding the individuals and organizations involved in this conspiracy is mind boggling, even for the most astute among us. Most people react with disbelief and skepticism towards the topic, unaware that they have been conditioned (brainwashed) to react with skepticism by institutional and media influences that were created by the Mother of All mind control organizations: The Tavistock Institute of Human Relations in London. Author and de-programmer Fritz Springmeier (The Top 13 Illuminati Bloodlines) says that most people have built in "slides" that short circuit the mind's critical examination process when it comes to certain sensitive topics. "Slides", Springmeier reports, is a CIA term for a conditioned type of response which dead ends a person's thinking and terminates debate or examination of the topic at hand. For example, the mention of the word "conspiracy" often solicits a slide response with many people. (Springmeier has co-authored three books on trauma-based programming which detail how the Illuminati employs highly tuned and extremely sophisticated Mind Control (MC) training programs that begin the programming process while the intended victim is still within the womb. Mind Control is a much greater problem than most people realize. According to Cisco Wheeler, a former Illuminati mind control programmer, there are 10 million people who have been programmed as mind controlled slaves using trauma-based MC programs with names like Monarch and MK Ultra.

The newer, non-trauma, electronic means of MC programming that grew out of the Montauk Project, may include millions more. Al Bielek, who played a principle role in the development of the Montauk Project, said that there likely 10 million victims of Montauk style mind control programming worldwide, the majority located in the USA. He also said that there are covert Montauk Programming 'Centers' in every major city in the U.S.)

What most Americans believe to be "Public Opinion" is in reality carefully crafted and scripted propaganda designed to elicit a desired behavioral response from the public. Public opinion polls are really taken with the intent of gauging the public's acceptance of the Illuminati's planned programs. A strong showing in the polls tells the Illuminati that the programing is "taking", while a poor showing tells the NWO manipulators that they have to recast or "tweak" the programming until the desired response is achieved. While the thrust and content of the propaganda is decided at Tavistock, implementation of the propaganda is executed in the United States by well over 200 'think tanks' such as the Rand Corporation and the Brookings Institute which are overseen and directed by the top NWO mind control organization in the United States, the Stanford Research Institute (SRI) in Menlo Park, California.

The NWO global conspirators manifest their agenda through the skillful manipulation of human emotions, especially fear. In the past centuries, they have repeatedly utilized a contrivance that NWO researcher and author David Icke has characterized in his latest book, The Biggest Secret, as Problem, Reaction, and Solution.

The technique is as follows: Illuminati strategists create the Problem- by funding , assembling, and training an "opposition" group to stimulate turmoil in an established political power (sovereign country, region, continent, etc.) that they wish to impinge upon and thus create opposing factions in a conflict that the Illuminati themselves maneuvered into existence. In recent decades, so called "opposition" groups are usually identified in the media as 'freedom fighters' or 'liberators' (recently the KLA-Kosovo Liberation Army).

At the same time, the leader of the established political power where the conflict is being orchestrated is demonized and, on cue, referred to as 'another Hitler' (take your pick: Saddam Hussein, Milosevic, Kadaffi, etc.). The 'freedom fighters' are not infrequently assembled from a local criminal element (i.e. KLA, drug traffickers). In the spirit of true Machiavellian deceit, the same NWO strategists are equally involved in covertly arming and advising the leader of the established power as well (the Illuminati always profits from any armed conflict by loaning money, arming, and supplying all parties involved in a war).

The conflict is drawn to the world stage by the controlled media outlets with a barrage of photos and video tape reports of horrific and bloody atrocities suffered by innocent civilians. The cry goes up "Something has to be done!" And That is the desired Reaction (note: the same technique is presently being used to bring about gun control in the United States).

The NWO puppeteers then provide the Solution by sending in UN 'Peace Keepers' (Bosnia) or a UN 'Coalition Force' (Gulf War) or NATO Bombers and then ground troops (Kosovo). Once installed, the 'peace keepers' never leave (Bosnia, Kosovo). The idea is to have NWO controlled ground troops in all major countries or strategic areas where significant resistance to the New World Order takeover is likely to be encountered.

East Timor, Indonesia. (9/14/99) Virtually , the same strategy used to occupy Kosovo with UN/NATO troops was applied by the NWO manipulators to take military control of East Timor. Once again, the same morality play is trotted out for public consumption: the local evil and demonic Indonesian Army trained militias responsible for the slaughter of innocent civilians following the August 30 vote for Independence (from Indonesian control), must be stopped at all costs. This time, Australia (to keep up the appearance of an 'international' humanitarian effort) will lead the charge with 'peacekeeping' troops. Of course, it didn't take long for Madeline Albright to announce that US 'support assets' will be part of the "UN Peacekeeping Team". In a front page story in the LA Times (9/13/99), Mike Jendrzejczyk of Human Rights Watch (an Illuminati front group) in Washington DC   said that it's "crucial" that "peacekeepers have the authority to disarm militia forces and any Indonesian soldiers actively working with them".]

The local, sovereign military force is either defeated (i.e. Yugoslavia) or, as in the case of the United States itself, replaced by foreign UN "Partnership For Peace" (PFP) troops who take over the jobs of US soldiers who have been sent overseas on 'peacekeeping' missions. In addition to being killed in ground conflicts on foreign soil, US military forces will likely be reduced in the next few years through disease induced attrition (i.e. from mandatory Anthrax Vaccinations required of all US military personnel). These vaccinations will, in all probability, eventually produce the symptoms of the so-called Gulf War Illness, which was acquired by a certain percentage of Gulf War soldiers who were given a "special" anthrax vaccine (intended by the Illuminati/CIA as a test run to ascertain how quickly (and fatally) the disease would progress with a substantial population of healthy young men and women).

The corporate portion of the NWO pyramid seems to be dominated by international bankers and the big pharmaceutical cartels, as well as other major multinational corporations. The Royal Family of England, namely Queen Elizabeth II and the House of Windsor, (who are, in fact, descendants of the German arm of European Royalty -the Saxe-Coburg-Gotha family-changed the name to Windsor in 1914), are high level players, along with the British oligarchy which controls the upper strata of the Illuminati. The decision making Illuminati nerve centers of this effort are in the London (especially the City of London), Basel Switzerland, and Brussels (NATO headquarters).

The United Nations, along with all the agencies working under the UN umbrella, such as the World

Health Organization (WHO), are full time players in this scheme. Similarly, NATO is a military tool of the NWO.

The leaders of all major industrial countries like the United States, England, Germany, Italy, Australia, New Zealand, etc. (E.g. members of the "G7/G8") are active and fully cooperative participants in this conspiracy. In this century, the degree of control exerted by the Illuminati has advanced to the point that only certain hand-picked individuals, who are groomed and selected by the Illuminati are even eligible to become the prime minister or president of countries like England, Germany, or The United States. It didn't matter whether Bill Clinton or Bob Dole won the Presidency in 1996, the results would have been the same (except maybe for Zipper Gate). Both men are playing on the same team for the same ball club. Anyone who isn't a team player is taken out: i.e.President Kennedy, Ali Bhutto (Pakistan) and Aldo Moro (Italy). More recently, Admiral Borda and William Colby were also killed because they were either unwilling to go along with the conspiracy to destroy America, weren't cooperating in some capacity, or were attempting to expose/ thwart the Takeover agenda.

Most of the major wars, political upheavals, and economic depression/recessions of the past 100 years (and earlier) were carefully planned and instigated by the machinations of these elites. They include The Spanish-American War (1898), World

War I and World War II; TheGreat Depression; the Bolshevik Revolution of 1917; the Rise of Nazi Germany; the Korean War; the Vietnam War; the 1989-91"fall" of Soviet Communism, the 1991 Gulf War; and the recent War in Kosovo. Even the French Revolution was an orchestrated into existence by the Barvaian Illuminati and the House of Rothchild.

One of the first US presidents to be associated with the NWO was Woodrow Wilson. He left little doubt as to who he was and why he was President.

Woodrow Wilson

Like Roosevelt before him, Woodrow Wilson regarded himself as the personal representative of the people. "No one but the President," he said, "seems to be expected ... to look out for the general interests of the country." He developed a program of progressive reform and <u>asserted international leadership in building a new world order.</u> In 1917 he proclaimed American entrance into World War I a crusade to make the world "<u>safe for democracy.</u>"

Wilson had seen the frightfulness of war. He was born in Virginia in 1856, the son of a Presbyterian minister who during the Civil War was a pastor in Augusta, Georgia, and during Reconstruction a professor in the charred city of Columbia, South Carolina.

After graduation from Princeton (then the College of New Jersey) and the University of Virginia Law School, Wilson earned his doctorate at Johns Hopkins University and entered upon an academic career. In 1885 he married Ellen Louise Axson.

Wilson advanced rapidly as a conservative young professor of political science and became president of Princeton in 1902.

His growing national reputation led some conservative Democrats to consider him Presidential timber. First they persuaded him to run for Governor of New Jersey in 1910. In the campaign he asserted his independence of the conservatives and of the machine that had nominated him, endorsing a *progressive* platform, which he pursued as governor.

He was nominated for President at the 1912 Democratic Convention and campaigned on a program called the New Freedom, which stressed individualism and states' rights. In the three-way election he received only 42 percent of the popular vote but an overwhelming electoral vote.

Wilson maneuvered through Congress three major pieces of legislation. The first was a lower tariff, the Underwood Act; *attached to the measure was a graduated Federal income tax.* The passage of the Federal Reserve Act provided the Nation with the more elastic money supply it badly needed. In 1914 antitrust legislation established a Federal Trade Commission to prohibit unfair business practices.

Another burst of legislation followed in 1916. One new law prohibited child labor; another limited railroad workers to an eight-hour day. By virtue of this legislation and the slogan "he kept us out of war," Wilson narrowly won re-election.

But after the election Wilson concluded that America could not remain neutral in the World War. On April 2,1917, he asked Congress for a declaration of war on Germany.

Massive American effort slowly tipped the balance in favor of the Allies. Wilson went before Congress in January 1918, to enunciate American war aims-- the Fourteen Points, the last of which would establish "A general association of nations...affording mutual guarantees of political independence and territorial integrity to great and small states alike."

After the Germans signed the Armistice in November 1918, Wilson went to Paris to try to build an enduring peace. He later presented to the

Senate the Versailles Treaty, containing the Covenant of the League of Nations, and asked, "Dare we reject it and break the heart of the world?" But the election of 1918 had shifted the balance in Congress to the Republicans. By seven votes the Versailles Treaty failed in the Senate.

The President, against the warnings of his doctors, had made a national tour to mobilize public sentiment for the treaty. Exhausted, he suffered a stroke and nearly died. Tenderly nursed by his second wife, Edith Bolling Galt, he lived until 1924.

President Woodrow Wilson 1916 *"I am a most unhappy man. I have unwittingly ruined my country. A great industrial nation is controlled by its system of credit. Our system of credit is concentrated. The growth of the nation, therefore, and all our activities are in the hands of a few men. We have come to be one of the worst ruled, one of the most completely controlled and dominated governments in the civilized world. No longer a government by free opinion, no longer a government by conviction and the vote of the majority, but a government by the opinion and duress of a small group of dominant men."*

President Franklin Roosevelt Nov. 21, 1933 *"The real truth of the matter is, as you and I know, that a financial element in the larger centers has owned the government since the days of Andrew Jackson."*

Franklin Delano Roosevelt

The All-Seeing Eye, The President, The Secretary and The Guru
- by Terry Melanson ©, July 2001
"Wallace's reasons for wanting to introduce the Great Seal onto the American currency were based on his belief that America was reaching a turning point in her history and that great spiritual changes were imminent. He believed that the 1930s represented a time when a great spiritual awakening was going to take place which would precede the creation of the one-world state."

- Michael Howard, The Occult Conspiracy, p.95

If you live in the United States of America, then from the time you become conscious of money, the Great Seal becomes a part of your psyche – whether you realize it or not. Moreover, since U.S. dollars are, in effect, standard international currency, this Great Seal infiltrates the minds of men the world over – both free and bond.

The centerpiece of this mandala is the All-Seeing Eye – an important symbol within freemasonry and rosicrucian traditions for hundreds of years. So it is not surprising to find pride among occultists who understand the significance of this emblem: "Our beautiful seal is an expression of Freemasonry, an expression of occult ideas." (Wyckoff, H. S. The Great American Seal. The Mystic Light, the Rosicrucian Magazine, p.56) 1

The first attempts at including the All-Seeing Eye on the seal were not successful. The first die of the Great Seal was cut from brass in 1782. In 1825, 1841, 1877, 1885, and 1902, new dies were cut, but each time the reverse went uncut and unused . . . the Illuminati's plan for the New World Order had not been advanced far enough, yet, to be announced.

The New World Order is an expression that has been used by illuminized Freemasonry since the days of Weishaupt to signify the coming world government. "It is necessary to establish a universal regime over the whole world", Weishaupt had said. (Writings of the Illuminati, 1780)

During the first part of the 20th century and up to the time the reverse of the seal was first used, a series of victories over the sovereignty of the United States had already been won. Illuminist agents committed to the one-world interests of the Rothschild-Warburg-Rockefeller cartel had accomplished some important stepping stones to this New World Order: Federal Reserve System (1913); League of Nations (1920); Royal Institute of International Affairs, and Council on Foreign Relations (1920-21); and the Stock Market Crash of 1929. The consolidation of power was complete and the reverse side of the seal, which remained largely unknown to the American people for more than 150 years, could now be placed.

The Intervention by the Masonic-Rosicrucian-Illuminati In 1934, Secretary of Agriculture, soon-to-be Vice-President (1940-44) and 32nd degree freemason Henry Wallace submitted a proposal to the president to mint a coin depicting the seal's obverse and reverse. President Franklin D Roosevelt, also a 32nd degree freemason, liked the idea but opted to instead place it on the dollar bill. According to Henry Wallace, in a letter dated February 6, 1951, "the Latin phrase Novus Ordo Seclorum impressed me as meaning the 'New Deal' of the Ages."

"Roosevelt as he looked at the colored reproduction of the Seal was first struck with the representation of the 'All-Seeing Eye,' a Masonic representation of Great Architect the Universe. Next he was impressed with the idea that the foundation for the new order of the ages had been laid in 1776 (May 1st, 1776, founding of the Illuminati) but would be completed only under the eye of the Great Architect. Roosevelt like myself was a 32nd degree Mason. He suggested that the Seal be put on the dollar bill rather that a coin."

Besides being a high ranking freemason and having the distinction of introducing socialism into the American political system, <u>Roosevelt was a member of a secret society</u> called the Ancient Arabic Order of Nobles of the Mystics Shrine (Shriners), attaining the grade of a Knight of Pythias. The Order of Nobles and Mystics claimed to be an offshoot of the Illuminati.

Freemasons, Walter Flemming and William Florence founded an American branch in New York, 1872. Membership in the order was open only to Freemasons who had reached the 32nd degree of the Ancient and Accepted Scottish Rite or those who've attained the last degree of the York Rite, the thirteenth degree (Knight Templar).

The Order of Nobles and Mystics have origins which date back to the seventh century — apparently founded by a descendent of

Mohammed. Author Michael Howard describes the Order's symbols.

"The symbol of the Order is a crescent moon, made from the claws of a Bengal tiger, engraved with a pyramid, an urn and a pentagram. The crescent is suspended from a scimitar and in the Order is a representation of the Universal Mother worshipped in ancient times as Isis. The horns of the crescent point downwards because it represents the setting moon of the old faith at the rising of the Sun of the new religion of the brotherhood of humanity."
- The Occult Conspiracy, p.93

According to Anton LaVey, founder of the Church of Satan, Roosevelt's Shriner's have a ritual similar to a satanic ritual called "The Ceremony of the Stifling Air", or better known as "L'air Epais." LaVey says that this rite was originally performed "when entering the sixth degree of the Order of the Knights Templar." Remember that if the Masonic candidate chooses to follow the York Rite, after he completes the 13th degree called the Knight Templar, he can apply to become a Shriner.
LaVey describes the Templars' ritual thus:

"The original Templars' rite of the Fifth degree symbolically guided the candidate through the Devil's Pass in the mountains separating the East from the West (the Yezidi domain). At the fork of the trail the candidate would make an important decision: either to retain his present identity, or strike out on the Left-Hand Path to Shambhala, where he might dwell in Satan's household, having rejected the foibles and hypocrisies of the everyday world.

A striking parallel to this rite is enacted within the mosques of the Ancient Arabic Order of the Nobles of the Mystic Shrine, an order reserved for thirty-second degree Masons. The Nobles have gracefully removed themselves from any implication of heresy by referring to the place beyond the Devil's Pass as the domain where they might "worship at the shrine of Islam."

Once the celebrant has taken this degree, he embarks upon the Left Hand Path and chooses Hell in place of Heaven."
- The Satanic Rituals — Companion to the Satanic Bible, p. 21
Pretty powerful stuff for sure, and not what you would expect of the "merry old men" wearing "fez-hats" and tending to burn victims!

One part of LaVey's interpretation I find interesting is the choice the candidate makes in following the "Left-Hand Path to Shambhala."

2 - In esoteric doctrine the principle city of the underground world is Shambhala.
In this subterranean kingdom presides an all-powerful and All-Seeing ruler – The King of the World. Some have called him Sanat Kumara

3, others, King Satan. This may not be as far fetched as it seems. The Bible clearly states that Satan is the "prince" and "lord" of this world – John 12: 31 & 14: 30, Eph. 6: 12, Luke 4: 6-7, and 2 Cor. 4: 4 – and in fact has dominion over this fallen world. This King of the World, according to Eastern tradition, has a rule and influence which stretches to the surface by means of trusted emissaries who carry out specific tasks and duties – including a secret 8 million who carry out his tasks unbeknownst to us all.

4 - As we shall see, one such "emissary" had a considerable influence with Roosevelt's Secretary of Agriculture.

Wallace's Occult Connections
Many of Henry Wallace's ideas originated with his guru, the Russian mystic and artist Nicholas Roerich. He was an adventurer/occultist in the tradition of Madame Blavatsky, Aleister Crowley and G. I. Gurdjieff. Roerich spent many years travelling through Nepal and Tibet studying with the lamas in the Buddhist monasteries of those countries. Roerich was searching for the lost city of Shambhala. In esoteric circles Shambhala is the home of the Ascended Masters, Secret Chiefs, or the Great White Brotherhood – the hidden hand behind the formation and guidance of Freemasons, the Sufis, the Knights Templars, the Rosicrucians, the Hermetic Order of the Golden Dawn and the

Theosophical Society – both Wallace and Roerich were members of the Theosophical Society, this is how Wallace met his Master.

Roerich seems to have been an emissary of sorts for the Great White Brotherhood – even bringing a mysterious stone to guide the League of Nations on behalf of the Masters. According to legend, the 'Chintamani Stone' was believed to be a part of a magical meteorite from a solar system in the Orion constellation. This Chintamani Stone is sent wherever a spiritual mission vital to humanity is set up, and is returned when that mission is completed.

5 - A mysterious stone was indeed mentioned by Wallace in one of his typical 'Dear Guru' letters to Roerich: "And I have thought of the admonition 'Await the Stone.' We await the Stone and we welcome you again to this glorious land of destiny." 6 Not surprisingly, occultists regard Roerich as the guiding hand behind the placement of America's Great Seal and the All-Seeing Eye, and matter-of-factly state that it was at Roerich's insistence that Wallace approach Roosevelt about finally printing the All-Seeing Eye on the dollar bill.

Henry Wallace was well versed in occult knowledge himself. In a letter to Roerich he stated, "the search – whether it be for the lost word of Masonry, or the Holy Chalice, or the potentialities of the age to come – is the one supremely worthwhile objective. All else is karmic duty. But surely everyone is a potential Galahad? So may we strive for the Chalice and the flame above it." The chalice he refers to, according to Michael Howard, is the Holy Grail, regarded by the Rosicrucians as a feminine symbol for perfection, and 'the age to come' is the dawning of the Aquarian Age. This I agree with, and further, "the age to come" is synonymous with Aleister Crowley's "New Age of Horus" – a Roerich occult contemporary. It seems that Novus Ordo Seclorum and Annuit Coeptis (He has blessed our beginning) has even deeper occult meanings than we're led to believe.

Illuminist Conspiracy?

Well, yes! These three "wise men" – by placing the reverse of the Great Seal on the dollar bill – succeeded in announcing to the world that America is on "the path", and is the world's best hope for the spiritual (occult) evolution of the planet. Considering how deep into the occult both Roosevelt and Wallace were already – and Wallace's connections to Theosophy – they had to of known that the most esteemed Theosophist of her time, Alice Bailey, had already declared that the Aquarian Age had begun in 1932. The whole symbology of the reverse is meant to be a mandala announcing this "New Age of Horus." They could not help but see the significance of this. And giving that their fellow illuminists in the Federal Reserve had now taken control of America's currency, it was a shoo-in.

As for Roerich, he was only doing the Hierarchy's bidding for he was also a channeler of the Ascended Master El Morya – a major avatar in the pantheon of Theosophy. Roerich, after his death, apparently succeeded in joining the Hierarchy, and has now become the occult equivalent of a catholic saint himself – an "Ascended Master." His messages are now channeled by Elizabeth Clare Prophet and one such message was "received", ironically enough, on October 28, 1990 at The Roosevelt Hotel.

"Symbolism is the language of the Mysteries ... By symbols men have ever sought to communicate to each other those thoughts which transcend the limitations of language. Rejecting man-conceived dialects as inadequate and unworthy to perpetuate divine ideas, the Mysteries thus chose symbolism as a far more ingenious and ideal method of preserving their transcendental knowledge. In a single figure a symbol may both reveal and conceal, for to the wise the subject of the symbol is obvious, while to the ignorant the figure remains inscrutable. Hence, he who seeks to unveil the secret doctrine of antiquity must search for that doctrine not upon the open pages of books which might fall into the hands of the unworthy but in the place where it was originally concealed."
— Manly P. Hall, The Secret Teachings of All Ages, p. 20

"These considerations lead us to an interesting topic, the Eye of Mind or the Eye of Horus ... and conveying the idea of the 'All seeing Eye'. The end set before the Egyptian neophyte was illumination, that is to be 'brought to light'. The Religion of Egypt was the Religion of the Light."

Thomas Milton Stewart, Symbolism of the Gods of the Egyptians and The Light They Throw on Freemasonry, London, England, Baskerville Press, Ltd., 1927, p. 5

"On the reverse of our nation's Great Seal is an unfinished pyramid to represent human society itself, imperfect and incomplete. Above floats the symbol of the esoteric orders, the radiant triangle with its all-seeing eye. ... There is only one possible origin for these symbols, and that is the secret societies which came to this country 150 years before the Revolutionary War. ... There can be no question that the great seal was directly inspired by these orders of the human Quest, and that it set forth the purpose for this nation. ..."

- Manly P. Hall, The Secret Destiny of America, pp. 174, 181.

Federal Emergency Management Administration (FEMA)

From Ken Adachi's website: - Educate-Yourself - The Freedom of Knowledge, The Power of Thought © http://educate-yourself.org/nwo/ - In America, the Federal Emergency Management Administration (FEMA) was created in 1979 under Presidential Memorandum 32 authored for President Carter by Prof. Samuel P. Huntington, a Harvard professor and former FEMA Advisory Board chairman. Huntington wrote the Seminal Peace for the Trilateral Commission in the mid 70's, in which he criticized democracy and economic development as outdated ideas. As co-author of the book, Crisis in Democracy, Huntington wrote:

"We have come to recognize that there are potential desirable limits to economic growth. There are also potentially desirable limits to the indefinite extension of political democracy. A government which lacks authority will have little ability short of cataclysmic crisis to impose on its people the sacrifices which may be necessary."

Huntington's ideas were rewritten into National Security Decision Directive #47 (NSDD47), which was enacted in July 1982 by President Reagan. Treated as a passing footnote by the media, this law identified legitimate areas to be upgraded to maintain national defense, but it also laid the groundwork for Emergency Mobilization Preparedness, a plan under which existing socio/economic regulations or other legal constraints would be waived in the event of a national emergency. This plan was further strengthened in Public Law 101-647, signed by President Bush in November 1990. What it boils down to is this: in the event that the President declares a national emergency, for any reason (from major earthquakes to increased international tensions or economic /financial crisis of any stripe), FEMA can then, at their discretion, implement Executive Orders 10995 through 11005 (see below/bg). These Executive Orders permit a takeover by FEMA of local, state, and national governments and the suspension of constitutional guarantees. FEMA will have the authority to exert any sort of control that it deems necessary upon the American public. A trained National Police Force, formally referred to by the name of Multi Jurisdictional Task Force (MJTF), wearing black uniforms and composed of:

1. specially selected US military personnel

2. foreign military units carrying United Nations ID cards, and

3. specially trained existing police groups from larger metropolitan American cities.

These members of the MJTF will implement and enforce martial law under the direction and control of FEMA. The President and Congress are out of the loop

FEMA is the Trojan Horse by which the New World Order will implement overt, police-state control over the American populace.

And from a different website, an explanation of the specific Presidential Executive Orders that are mentioned in the above FEMA article, and how the Executive Order process has been abused as far back as the Civil War and continuing. A good brief history lesson which ends by bringing matters up to the present and what we are up against when these EO's are put into practice by FEMA.

PRESIDENTIAL EXECUTIVE ORDERS
http://pfa.topcities.com/execuative_orders.html
Presidential Executive Orders allow the President to administrate the business of the federal government. He has the responsibility to execute and carry out the lawful statutes and can require obedience of those subject to the federal government's jurisdiction. What is considered lawful under the Constitution, and what is being actually accomplished today are issues of considerable debate, as well they should be. Also, where the jurisdiction of the federal government applies and where it does not are equally debatable, as the sovereign states have jurisdiction over their citizenry.

Any Executive Order that is printed in the Federal Register and draws no objection from Congress within thirty days becomes law. It is as valid as a statute passed by Congress and signed by the President into legislative authority and is enforceable as executive law in the Code of Federal Regulations [CFRs]. This came about through a long train of executive abuse, and congressional "rubber-stamps" (many under dubious conditions), which extend back to the civil war era. The essence of existing conditions is that the balance of power as provided for in the Constitution, has been overturned.

President Roosevelt exceeded his Constitutional powers when he issued Proclamation 2039 on March 6, 1933, which placed the lawful money (gold) of the people under the control of the Commander-in-Chief as property of the federal government. This was, in effect a violation of his oath of office. Congress had not yet assembled to give consent to any emergency powers act, or to permit suspension of the Constitutional Rights of any American Citizens.

(No surprise, as Roosevelt was a 33rd degree Mason, too! It was during his Administration, in 1935, they decided to go ahead and "reveal themselves" by putting their NWO symbol on the back of the One Dollar bill. note by /bg)

Did the 73rd Congress, on March 9, 1933, as a committee of the whole, become a principal in constructive treason, when they passed an ex post facto bill, exonerating FDR's lawless act, and accepting the state of emergency and emergency powers act?

The 73rd Congress used the acts of an earlier Congress, the 37th, as a precedent, who on July 4, 1861, convened over four months after Lincoln's inauguration, after he had declared war, suspended Habeas corpus, etc., and "rubber- stamped" the Commander-in-Chief's actions. The exact language Congress used on July 4, 1861 was used again, by Congress, on March 9, 1933, in 12 USC 95(b). The 73rd Congress not only allowed President Roosevelt to seize the people's property, it effectively declared war on the people, by removing the "exclusion of domestic transactions by American citizens" clause from an older 1917 Act. In so doing, Congress forced American citizens into a new "legal status."

The "emergency" established by FDR in 1933 has been continued, under varying auspices, by every president since. On November 14, 1996, President Clinton, through extending executive order 12938, which he had first established in November of 1994, continued the current state of emergency and this abuse of power and overthrow of the Constitution.

There is no amendment to the constitution providing for this. The "acts" of congress, which provide for it, themselves are unconstitutional, as no power to fundamentally change the balance of powers provided for in the Constitution is provided outside of the amendment process. There are now over 12 thousand of these executive orders, many of which establish alternate government control under emergency conditions which they define, and under which we perpetually live. Here are a few of the most extreme ones:

Order # Description

10995 Seizure of communications, public or private in the U.S. (Radio, TV, newspapers)

10997 Seizure of power, petroleum, fuels & minerals within the U.S., public and private.

10998 Seizure of food supplies and resources and all farm land and equipment in the U.S.

10999 Seizure of highways and transportation, including cars, trucks & vehicles in the U.S.

11000 Allocation of U.S. citizens to work forces, including splitting families, in the U.S.

11001 Seizure of health & education functions and facilities, public and private in the U.S.

11002 Designates Post Master Gen'l to register all persons through their local Post Office.

11003 Seizure of airports and aircraft, commercial, public or private within the U.S.

11004 Relocation of communities and designating new population centers in the U.S.

11005 Seizure of railroads, waterways and storage facilities in the U.S.
11051 Federal Emergency Management Agency (FEMA) admins executive orders.
11490 Combines executive orders 10995-11005 and 11051 into a single executive order.
12148 Defines national emergency as disaster, unrest, invasion or economic crisis (any/all of which they themselves plan to create to give them the "excuse" to implement the police state./bg).
12919 Delegates the responsibilities within FEMA in implementing executive orders.
The executive orders are in the Federal Register and can be viewed by any American who takes the time to look and wade through them. These executive orders are the law of the land and can be implemented at any time at the discretion of the President alone, as the state of emergency exists.

An example of how executive orders can currently impact the way of life of any U.S. citizen was seen when President Clinton, by executive order, confiscated 1.8 million acres of Utah public and private land in the fall of 1996 and set it aside as a national monument. This placed 75% of Utah's planned energy production capacity (coal) after the year 2000 out of reach of that state. It also placed 25% of this nations "clean" coal reserve off limits for national use, forcing us to be dependant on foreign interest (who by the way were major contributors to President Clinton's re-election). It also resulted in two large counties becoming essentially "wards of the state" as the total government land owning in those counties is now over 99%. Is this the America our founding fathers envisioned? What would occur if a president initiated the executive orders described above on a broad basis as a pretext for assuming dictatorial powers in a fabricated emergency?

FEMA has constructed up to 80 large detention centers all over this country as a part of a 1989 presidential directive and as a part of the 1991 department of defense budget, and later budgets. They are complete and each is capable of holding 45,000+ individuals. This amounts to over 3.5 million individuals! Who are they for? These camps have been built for the "detention" (meaning imprisonment) of those who resist or violate the executive order state should it ever be implemented. What 20th century governments can you think of who have instituted similar programs? Three major ones come to mind Nazi Germany, the Soviet Union and China. When you couple this information with the reports of foreign troops training on U.S. soil by the tens of thousands over the last 4 years (figures range from 200,000 to 450,000) the potential implications are ominous. Source: http://groups.yahoo.com/group/ THE_PARADISE_REPORTER
[...]

The Trilateral Commission

President Jimmy Carter

The Trilateral Commission was established in 1973. Its founder and primary financial angel was international financier, David Rockefeller, longtime chairman of the Rockefeller family-controlled Chase Manhattan Bank and undisputed overlord of his family's global corporate empire.

Rockefeller's idea for establishing the commission emerged after he had read a book entitled Between

Two Ages written by an Establishment scholar, Prof. Zbigniew Brzezinski of Columbia University.

In his book Brzezinski proposed a vast alliance between North America, Western Europe and Japan. According to Brzezinski, changes in the modern world required it.

"Resist as it might," Brzezinski wrote elsewhere, "the American system is compelled gradually to accommodate itself to this emerging international context, with the U.S. government called upon to negotiate, to guarantee, and, to some extent, to protect the various arrangements that have been contrived even by private business."

In other words, it was necessary for the international upper class to band together to protect its interests, and to ensure, in the developed nations, that political leaders were brought to power who would ensure that the global financial interests (of the Rockefellers and the other ruling elites) would be protected over those of the hoi polloi.

POCANTICO HILLS CONFABS

Although the initial arrangements for the commission were laid out in a series of meetings held at the Rockefeller's famous Pocantico Hills estate outside New York City, Rockefeller first introduced the idea of the commission at an annual meeting of the Bilderberg group, this one held in Knokke, Belgium in the spring of 1972.

(The Bilderberg group is similar to the Trilateral Commission in that it is funded and heavily influenced by the Rockefeller empire, and composed of international financiers, industrialists, media magnates, union bosses, academics and political figures).

However, the much older Bilderberg group's membership is strictly limited to participants from the United States, Canada and Western Europe: i.e. the NATO alliance. For more on the Bilderberg group, keep an eye out for future stories in this paper.

The Trilateral Commission was unique, though, in that it brought the Japanese ruling elite into the inner councils of the global power brokers, a recognition of Japan's growing influence in the world economic and political arena.

RULING CLASSES UNITE

"The Commission's purpose is to engineer an enduring partnership among the ruling classes of North America, Western Europe and Japan -- hence the term 'Trilateral' -- in order to safeguard the interests of Western capitalism in an explosive world. The private commission is attempting to mold public policy and construct a framework for international stability in the coming decades.

"To put it simply, Trilateralists are saying: The people, governments and economies of all nations must serve the needs of multinational banks and corporations.

"In short, Trilateralism is the current attempt by ruling elites to manage both dependence and democracy -- at home and abroad."

Another Trilateral critic, now-retired Sen. Barry Goldwater (R-Ariz.), views the commission as a Rockefeller family operation through and through. According to Goldwater:

"The Trilateral organization created by David Rockefeller was a surrogate -- the members selected by Rockefeller, its purposes defined by Rockefeiler, its funding supplied by Rockefeller. David Rockefeller screened and selected every individual who was invited to participate."

PICKING POLICYMAKERS

David Rockefeller and Brzezinski then began the process of selecting from among the "Trilateral" nations the several hundred elite power brokers who would be permitted to join in Trilateral policymaking in the coming years.

One of the commission's primary goals was to place a Trilateral-influenced president in the White House in 1976, and to achieve that goal it was necessary to groom an appropriate candidate who would be willing to cooperate with Trilateral aims.

Rockefeller and Brzezinski selected a handful of well-known liberal Democrats and a scattering of

Republicans (primarily of the liberal-internationalist bent) to serve on the commission.

And in an effort to give regional balance to the commission Rockefeller invited the then-obscure one-term Democratic governor of Georgia, Jimmy Carter, to join the commission.

ROCKEFELLER CENTER SOUTH
Rockefeller had longtime ties to the local Atlanta political and economic Establishment. In fact, much of Rockefeller's personal investment portfolio is in Atlanta real estate. (According to David Horowitz, co-author of The Rockefellers, "Atlanta is Rockefeller Center South.")

And Rockefeller himself had once even invited Carter to dine with him at the Chase Manhattan Bank several years before, as early as 1971, the year Carter began serving as governor.

Carter very definitely impressed Rockefeller and Brzezinski, more so than another Southern Democrat, Florida Gov. Reuben Askew, also selected to serve on the commission and viewed, like Carter, as a possible Trilateral candidate.

In fact, according to Brzezinski, "It was a close thing between Carter and Askew, but we were impressed that Carter had opened up trade offices for the state of Georgia in Brussels and Tokyo. That seemed to fit perfectly into the concept of the Trilateral."

Carter, in fact, like Askew, did announce for the 1976 Democratic presidential nomination, but because of Rockefeller's interest, Carter had the inside shot.

So much so that in a speech at the commission's first annual meeting in Kyoto, Japan in May of 1975, Rockefeller's man Brzezinski promoted the then-still obscure Carter to his fellow Trilateralists as an ideal presidential candidate.

CUT AND DRIED
From that point on, it was all cut and dried. According to Goldwater: "Rockefeller and Brzezinski found Carter to be their ideal candidate. They helped him win the Democratic nomination and the presidency.

"To accomplish this purpose they mobilized the money-power of the Wall Street bankers, the intellectual influence of the academic community -- which is subservient to the wealth of the great tax-free foundations -- and the media controllers represented in the membership of the CFR and the Trilateralists."

(The aforementioned Council on Foreign Relations -- is another Rockefeller-financed foreign policy pressure group similar to the Trilateralists and the

Bilderberg group, although the CFR is composed solely of American citizens.)

(In his book The Carter Presidency and Beyond, published in 1980 by the Ramparts Press, Prof. Laurence H. Shoup devotes an entire chapter to demonstrating how the Trilateral-linked and Trilateral-controlled Establishment media promoted the presidential candidacy in 1976 of the then-obscure Georgia Gov. Jimmy Carter.)

Carter, of course, campaigned as a "populist" -- as a "man of the people" -- as an "outsider" with no ties to the Establishment. The fact is, however, Carter, who said he'd never lie, was an elitist, an insider, the Trilateral Commission's "man on the white horse."

And with the power of the commission and the Rockefeller empire and its media influence behind him, Carter made his way to the presidency, establishing the first full-fledged Trilateral administration, appointing numerous Trilateralists to key policymaking positions and carrying out the Trilateral agenda to the hilt.

President George Bush in a speech to Congress on SEPTEMBER 11, (9/11) 1990, SAID THIS: "[The war in Iraq is] a rare opportunity to move toward an historic period of cooperation. Out of these troubled times...a New World Order can emerge."

In his September 21, 1992 speech to the United Nations, President George Bush announced that foreign troops, would occupy America and train for a New World Order Army. He stated:

"Nations should develop and train military units for possible U.N. peacekeeping operations. ... If multinational units are to work together, they must train together. ... Effective multinational action will also require coordinated command & control and inter-operability of both equipment and communications." New World Order and E.L.F. Psychotronic Tyranny

The Term New World Order Now Changed into Global

Official Term of the New World Order
"A supranational authority to regulate world commerce and industry; an international organization that would control the production and consumption of oil; an international currency that would replace the dollar; a world development fund that would make funds available to free and communist nations alike; an international police force to enforce the edicts of the New World Order" (McAlvany Intelligence Advisory)

The drive of the Rockefellers and their allies is to create a one-world government combining super-capitalism and Communism under the same tent, all under their control...Do I mean conspiracy? Yes I do. I am convinced there is such a plot, international in scope, generations old in planning, and incredibly evil in intent. (Congressman Larry P. McDonald, 1976) In 1981 Congressmen McDonald calls for comprehensive congressional investigation of the CFR and Trilateral Commission. Congress is urged to investigate these organizations. Congressman McDonald was killed in the Korean

Airlines 747 that was shot down by the Soviets in 1983

Zep Tepi / The First Time of Osiris / The Golden Age / A New Order of the Ages / Novus Ordo Seclorum / New World Order / Globalization.

Different names, same agenda. It is the restoration of that corrupt "Golden Age" of incarnate demons which the Egyptian mystery religion represented and continues to represent. It is an ancient violent and immoral world which developed before the Flood which New Age spirit guides are seeking to re-establish, but which will be swept away by the War of Armageddon. The term "Golden Age" is a very misleading one, as is the term "spirituality" when used in conjunction with Adam Weishaupt whose "spirituality" was referred to as "horrifying." The Illuminati's fundamental principles pervert the noble meaning of spirituality, and are working for the establishment of a "horrifying" "Golden Age." New Age Army Expose, Psychic Warrior Subversion Exposed
See For Yourself - Selected Elites & Their NWO Affiliations

WASHINGTON — Treasury Secretary Paul O'Neill said Sunday that the country is "on the edge of a golden age of prosperity," describing the current economic slowdown as an "adjustment period."

"If we do not follow the dictates of our inner moral compass and stand up for human life, then his lawlessness will threaten the peace and democracy of the emerging new world order we now see, this long dreamed-of vision we've all worked toward for so long." -- President George Bush (January 1991)

The New World Order program has been on the drawing board for many decades, despite denials and smears from the proponents, the insidious world domination and control preparations continue being set in place, the secretive terms of One World, New World Order, New International Economic Order etc have now been replaced with the more public term of Globalization.

In hundreds of books, articles, and speeches in the 20th century, many influential and powerful people, including many in Congress, have called for a New World Order, and the surrender of U.S. sovereignty and individual freedoms to a one world government, usually involving the U.N. military and the transfer of it to a one world U.N. army. TREASON: THE NEW WORLD ORDER By Author Gurudas

"Lets forgive the Nazi war criminals" (George Bush, New York Times, April, 14, 1990)

1993 December 20. George Bush was knighted by the Queen on as a Knight Grand Cross of the Most Honorable Order of the Bath. This was for his leadership in the Gulf War, when he sent American solders to die for England's interest of their petroleum in Kuwait. Order Of The Garter

Circumstantial evidence suggesting that then vice-president George Bush may have been involved with the attempt on the life of former President Reagan... the close connections between the family of convicted would-be assassin John Hinckley and the Bush family as well as Hinckley's Nazi background. David Emory's Talk Radio (On NAZIs)

I personally have learned of a few related incidents. I have come across reports of National Guardsmen undergoing specialized house-to-house search and seizure training and urban warfare tactics. I was also told that two men who managed to sneak into a Federal military plane 'graveyard' outside of Phoenix, Arizona had came across several freight train box-cars in which they discovered what they estimated to be from 2 to 3 million brand-new SHACKLES that were apparently being stored there, just waiting to be used! Civil War Is About To Begin In The United States

The extent of the American Government's [the corporate fascist military-industrial 'government' as opposed to the Constitutional or electorate 'government'] betrayal of her citizens can be further evidenced in the fact that these Chinese and Russian forces are RECEIVING PAYMENT FOR THEIR PRE-INVASION ACTIVITIES THROUGH THE INTERNATIONAL MONETARY FUND...

ISSUED ON AMERICAN GOVERNMENT CHECKS. In anticipation of the coming invasion from Russia and China [and German - U.N forces, etc.] Canada has even gone so far as to disband its Western Coast Guard Division, thus they are open to amphibious invasion of America from the West. This was openly evidenced recently through the presentation of a documentary report over the BBC television in London which detailed amphibious assault forces practicing war maneuvers and strategy in the Formosa Straits. When BBC newsmen were permitted to interview these soldiers in training, they repeatedly asked them the following question. "What are you preparing to use this training for?" The shocking, consistent reply was "FOR THE COMING INVASION OF AMERICA!" When it became clear that a gaff in security was created by airing this broadcast over television in England, its scheduled re-broadcast for the next day in London was hastily canceled. The Final Invasion Of The United States

1983 Peter Hoagland, Nebraska State Senator and Humanist, speaking on radio in 1983 with the great American Pastor and Patriot Everett Silevan said: "Fundamental, Bible believing people do not have the right to indoctrinate their children in their religious beliefs because we, the state, are preparing them for the year 2000, when America will be part of a one world global society and their children will not fit in."

As I walked through the crowd toward Reagan, I saw familiar faces associated with the "Order of the Rose." ("The Order of the Rose" was an emblem of those ushering in the New World Order. "Orders from the Rose" were orders from George Bush.) Across the room, Bill and Bob Bennett were laughing with Dick Cheney. Then Governor of Pennsylvania. Dick Thornburgh was engaged in conversation with Arlen Spector. Within the farthest reaches of my expanded peripheral vision, I saw George Bush talking with his U.N. confidant Madeleine Albright. (Reagan first introduced me to U.N. Ambassador Madeleine Albright as "my mentor" in Jesuit operations in the Caribbean.) Knowing I could see him as though I had eyes in the back of my head, Bush subtly signaled me to join them. "You know Madeleine Albright," Bush began. Expertly using terminology from previously instilled Catholic Jesuit beliefs, he continued, "She's the reverend mother of all sisters (slaves). She's so close to God that an order from her is an order from him." Albright snickered, apparently impressed with Bush's "witty" manipulation of program verbiage. "She rose in the U.N. through me to implement the New World peace process." (Trance Formation of America, The true life story of a CIA Mind Control Slave by Cathy O'Brien, pg 176)

According to some insiders, the New World Order would already be history if they didn't fear the possibility of an honest & constitutional U.S. Military. http://www.militarycorruption.com/

The Judas attitude of the Administration is symbolized in an article written by Bill Clinton's very close friend, Deputy Secretary of State Strobe Talbott, titled: "The Birth of the Global Nation." Talbott strongly attacked American national sovereignty, stating: "NATIONAL AS WE KNOW IT WILL BE OBSOLETE: ALL STATES WILL RECOGNIZE A SINGLE, GLOBAL" (666) "AUTHORITY," (7\20/92 Time Magazine).

The Zionists—the Jesuits are the Great Zionists. They control all of the historical High Zionists— Theodor Herzl, David Ben-Gurion, Golda Meir. Zionism is a Masonic term, coined by the Jesuits. They are the rulers; they are the Protocols; they are the Elders of Zion. So the Zionists are, indeed, evil and wicked; but they are controlled by Rome. The Jews are not all Zionists. Black Pope

The foreign troops are coming, which was the goal of Oslo to begin with. At Genoa, today, Bush agreed to bring the UN-NATO troops to Israel. Tomorrow he meets the pope to sanctify the end of Israel's hegemony. Tonight three Arabs were murdered by "Jews," which is short for "Shabak." The troops, we will be told, will protect both sides from violent murder. The New World Order arrives in Israel and very soon. (Barry Chamish)

The goal of the CFR was to influence all aspects of society in such a way that one day Americans would wake up and find themselves in a ONE NEW WORLD SYSTEM "whether they liked it or not." Their hope was to get Americans to the point where entering a world government would seem natural and so that they would blink and miss what it is their naked eyes were truly seeing.   LUCIFER'S Network: Master's Of The New World Order

In the last fifty years Big Brother has been able to slowly erode the basic freedoms of all American citizens by hiding behind such cliché's as " national security risk " to throw innocent people in prison with the most flimsy, if not fabricated evidence. When the government claims that a case involves a national security threat, it's power increases tremendously. Government investigators have the power to:
1. Order wire taps or a search without a warrant.
2. Restrict the discovery of evidence to who may see it.
3. Impede the accessed defense lawyers access to their client or require that an entire jury have security clearance.
4. In short, they can throw you in jail for as long as they wish too with any false or fabricated accusation against you.

But none of the wicked shall understand [that the End of the Age is upon them]." [Daniel 12:10

Unfortunately, what many so-called religious authorities fail to tell when arguing against self-defense by quoting this bit of scripture is that there are several words in the Hebrew language which express the verb "kill." The Hebrew word used in this commandment ALWAYS means "murder" and ONLY in what would now be called a "pre-meditated" murder at that.

Unfortunately, the word "kill" has changed since the time of King James when the first major translation of the Bible into English was carried out. The "kill" would more properly be translated as "murder" as far as modern English usage is concerned and, in fact, many modern translations of the Bible generally use "murder" in this passage. Check it out in a modern language translation of the Bible or-- better yet--with someone who knows Hebrew.

This Bible passage deals with murder, not self-defense and it's a grave mistake to interpret is as prohibiting self-defense. Thus the commandment is simply "Thou shalt not MURDER." (And any religious leader using this as an argument against self-defense should be dismissed as a liar or sent back for more theological training.) <u>PRAISE THE LORD AND (PLEASE DO) PASS THE AMMUNITION</u> A must read

The Bilderbergers

Even though many still deny their very existence, the fact is... in 1954 the most powerful men in the world met for the first time under the auspices of the Dutch royal crown and the Rockefeller family in the luxurious Hotel Bilderberg of the small Dutch town of Oosterbeck. For an entire weekend they debated the future of the world. When it was over, they decided to meet once every year to exchange ideas and analyze international affairs.

They named themselves the Bilderberg Club. Since then, they have gathered yearly in a luxurious hotel somewhere in the world arrogantly plotting the subversion and silent takeover of constitutional governments everywhere. Their goal is a World Government run exclusively by their hand-picked puppets.

Bilderberg founding member and, for 30 years, a steering committee member, Denis Healey said, "To say we were striving for a one-world government is exaggerated, but not wholly unfair. Those of us in Bilderberg felt we couldn't go on forever fighting one another for nothing and killing people and rendering millions homeless. So we felt that a single community throughout the world would be a good thing."

Shrewd and calculating, their hearts are filled with lust for power and consumed by greed for money.

Rich and aristocratic, they despise Christians and they loathe the lowly working class. They control the world's press and virtually all our banks and financial institutions. They screen and choose who America's leaders will be and even determine who will run on the Democratic and Republican Party tickets.

Among the elitist membership or attendees at Bilderberg meetings is David Rockefeller, Henry Kissinger, Lloyd Bentsen, Helmut Kohl, Prince Charles, Prince Juan Carlos I of Spain, Queen Beatrix of the Netherlands, Katharine Graham, Alice Rivlin, Gerald Ford, Bill and Hillary Clinton, Dan Quayle, Donald Rumsfeld, Colin L. Powell, John Edwards, Bill Bradley, Bill Richardson, Christopher Dodd, Dianne Feinstein, Kathleen Sebelius, Alexander Haig, Ralph E. Reed, George Stephanopoulos, William J McDonough (former president of the Federal Reserve Bank of New York), U.S. Treasury Secretary Timothy F. Geithner, George Soros, Paul Volcker & Alan Greenspan (former Chairman of the Federal Reserve), Federal Reserve Chairman Ben Bernanke, World Bank president Robert Zoellick, H. J. Heinz II (CEO of H. J. Heinz Company), Peter A. Thiel (Co-Founder, PayPal),

Eric E. Schmidt (Chairman and Chief Executive Officer, Google), Lloyd Blankfein (CEO of Goldman Sachs), Rupert Murdoch, Donald E. Graham (Chairman of the Board of The Washington Post

Company), William F. Buckley, Jr. (founder of National Review and former host of Firing Line), Peter Jennings, George Will, Lesley Stahl, Bill D. Moyers, and many others. The list includes prominent persons in politics, the military, financial institutions, major corporations, academia, and the media.

Leaders of the Bilderberg Club argue that discretion is necessary to allow participants in the debates to speak freely without being on the record or reported publicly. Wikipedia recently deleted the Bilderberg attendees list, citing it to be possibly defamatory towards living persons.

Why are the Davos World Economic Forum and G8 meetings carried in every newspaper, given front page coverage, with thousands of journalists in attendance, while no one covers Bilderberg Club meetings even though they are annually attended by Presidents of the International Monetary Fund, The World Bank, Federal Reserve, chairmen of 100 most powerful corporations in the world such as DaimlerChrysler, Coca Cola, British Petroleum, Chase Manhattan Bank, American Express, Goldman Sachs, Microsoft, Vice Presidents of the United States, Directors of the CIA and the FBI, General Secretaries of NATO, American Senators and members of Congress, European Prime Ministers and leaders of opposition parties, top editors and CEOs of the leading newspapers in the world.

"We are grateful to the Washington Post, The New York Times, Time Magazine and other great publications whose directors have attended our meetings and respected their promises of discretion for almost forty years. It would have been impossible for us to develop our plan for the world if we had been subjected to the lights of publicity during those years. But, the world is now more sophisticated and prepared to march towards a world government. The supranational sovereignty of an intellectual elite and world bankers is surely preferable to the national auto-determination practiced in past centuries." -- David Rockefeller

The Trilateral Commission

The Trilateral Commission sprang from the Bilderbergers when one of its principal members, Esso or Standard Oil's David Rockefeller came into conflict with his fellows over whether to include Japan in the club.

Upon reading the 1970 book Between Two Ages, David Rockefeller lured its writer, Professor Zbigniew Brzezinski, away from Columbia University to become the Chairman and co-founder of the Trilateral Commission in 1973. Brzezinski, who later became the mastermind of Jimmy Carter's foreign affairs and national security blunders, is still looked to as a policy guru by the liberal media today. Using the same collectivist mindset, objectives and premise as the CFR, Rockefeller funded and set up the New York-based Trilateral Commission with Zbigniew Brzezinski as its intellectual architect and purposely patterned after Brzezinski's book.

Along with Zbigniew Brzezinski and a few others, including the Brookings Institution, Council on Foreign Relations and the Ford Foundation, Rockefeller convened initial meetings and held their first executive committee meeting in Tokyo in October 1973. Members include corporate CEOs, politicians of all major parties, distinguished academics, university presidents, labor union leaders and not-for-profits involved in overseas philanthropy.

The Trilateral Commission was founded to become a type of international CFR. The goal of the Trilateral Commission is to align the free world with the advanced communist states to organize a world government. [Eric Barger, "The New World Order Under Clinton: Establishment Insiders and Political Deceit," The Christian World Report, May 1993, pg. 7.]

Members of the Trilateral Commission were instrumental in creating the European Union as well. The EU is the prototype of global governance that will soon exert its influence to reshuffle world relationships.

Some people who are or have been members include:
David Rockefeller: Founder of the Commission; Chairman of the Chase Manhattan Bank board from 1969 to 1981; Chairman of the Council on Foreign Relations from 1970 to 1985, now honorary Chairman; a life member of the Bilderberg Group.
Presidents George H.W. Bush, Jimmy Carter, and Bill Clinton
Dick Cheney, William Cohen, Dianne Feinstein, David Gergen, Henry Kissinger
Federal Reserve Chairmen Alan Greenspan and Paul Volcker

Caspar Weinberger: Secretary of Defense under Reagan
Yotaro Kobayashi, (chairman of the Fuji Xerox company),
John H. Bryan (former CEO of Sara Lee bakeries, affiliated with the World Economic Forum and part of the Board for Sara Lee, Goldman Sachs, General Motors, British Petroleum and Bank One).

Due to Goldman Sachs secretive culture and revolving door relationship with the Federal government, Goldman has recently been referred to as Wall Street's secret society, with former Goldman employees currently heading the New York Stock Exchange, the World Bank, the U.S. Treasury Department, the White House staff, and even rival firms such as Merrill Lynch. Its landmark profits during the 2007 Subprime mortgage financial crisis led the New York Times to proclaim that Goldman Sachs is without peer in the world of finance.

James E. Burke (CEA of Johnson & Johnson from 1976 to 1989)

Hank Greenberg (former chairman and CEO of American International Group (AIG), the world's largest insurance and financial services corporation). It should come as no surprise that when AIG faced huge investment losses that threatened its solvency in 2008, the American government stepped in with billions of dollars of taxpayer money to keep the company afloat.

Lee Raymond (ExxonMobil (Former CEO and Chairman, vice chairman of the Board of Trustees of the American Enterprise Institute, director of J.P. Morgan Chase & Co., director and member of the Executive Committee and Policy Committee of the American Petroleum Institute), and others.

Close Connections to Banking Industry

The economic chaos in the world today is a direct result of policies set in motion to foster a New International Economic Order (NIEO), according to Patrick Wood writing in the August Review. The NIEO was the explicit creation of the Trilateral Commission, founded by David Rockefeller and Zbigniew Brzezinski in 1973, and their early papers and task force reports clearly asserted their NIEO plans.

Actions taken by the Trilateral Commission generally help the banking industry. Jeremiah Novak, writing in the July 1977 issue of Atlantic, said that after international oil prices rose when Nixon set price controls on American domestic oil, many developing countries were required to borrow from banks to buy oil, many of them with doubtful repayment abilities. All told, private multinational banks, particularly Rockefeller's Chase Manhattan, have loaned nearly $52 billion to developing countries. An overhauled IMF would provide another source of credit for these nations, and would take the big private banks off the hook.This proposal is the cornerstone of the Trilateral plan.

There is mounting evidence, according to Wood, that there is a plan underway to corner the global supply of gold, thus laying the groundwork for a global currency exclusively controlled by Trilaterals and their friends. By extension, economic and political mechanisms would be controlled to the same extent. From a Trilateral perspective, the Bretton Woods system had two flaws: Gold was rapidly being decentralized into non-Trilateral hands and it limited the arbitrary creation of paper money to finance projects launched by Trilateral-related global companies. Since 1973, there has been an overarching plan to quietly centralize gold into private hands, using incrementally created wealth made possible by rapidly inflating paper currencies. In 1976, Antony Sutton wrote, "The assault on gold today is an integral part of a planned move into a new economic order under the dominance of a single country. It was Nazi Germany in the 1940's; it is the United States in the 1970's. In brief, the war on gold that we observe today, and discuss below, is dollar imperialism, designed to maintain the U.S. dollar as the only world currency without competitors. The purpose is the formation of a world totalitarian state under Wall Street dominance." (The War on Gold, Antony C. Sutton, 1976, p. 63)

Learn more about the Trilateral Commission
Trilateral Commission: World Shadow Government
In Jason Bermas' film, Invisible Empire is all conspiracy and no theory – proving beyond doubt how the elite have openly conspired to insidiously rule the globe via the engines of the CFR, the United Nations, the Trilateral Commission, and the Bilderberg group.

INTERNATIONAL BANKERS, TOP GLOBALISTS, HEADS OF NEW WORLD ORDER.

In order of importance:

Rothschild family

Warburg family

Schiff family

Oppenheimer family

Royal Family of England

Saxe-Coburg-Gotha family

Rockefeller family

Morgan family

Harriman family

Carnegie family

Rothschild is by far the most influential, holding approximately half of all the worlds wealth. That family is directly responsible for founding most of the other families or helping them get up off their feet.

The Rothschild philosophy:

1) Law is force in disguise. Right lies in force ("Might makes Right") The right to rule lies in force.

2) Political freedom is an idea, not a fact. In order to usurp political power, all that is necessary is to preach 'liberalism,' and the electorates will give up more and more power to the conspirators.

3) Money is all powerful. Governments are insignificant compared to money. Since governments control the money, that control must be removed from governments, and put in the hands of the conspirators.

4) Any and all means to achieve the goal of world domination by the conspirators is justified.

5) The size, scope, and power of the conspirators' resources must remain hidden.

6) Alcohol, drugs, and moral corruption shall be used to weaken the will of the people.

7) Wars should be instigated and orchestrated so that both sides would be in their debt (in other

words, the conspirators would gain profit and power, no matter who "won" the wars!).

8 Propaganda and control of information should be used to influence opinion.

9) Pre-planned and artificially manipulated financial panics and depression should be used to tame the people, and weaken governments, so as to ultimately form a one-world government, with the conspirators as the rulers.

The "Rothschild Formula" for NWO as Edward Griffin, author of Creature From Jekyll Island, puts it:

1) War is the ultimate discipline to any government. Survival from war becomes primary - everything else is secondary.

2) All that is necessary to insure government indebtedness (to the international banking conspiracy) is war - or the threat of war.

3) To create such a situation, it is necessary to pit two countries (or segments of one country) of equal force against one another - or to create them (the two opposing countries or segments of one country) if they do not already exist. ("Pit one side against the other, and finance both sides - so that the bankers win, no matter which side actually "wins.").

4) The ultimate obstacle to this formula is a country that is not willing to finance war through debt. When this occurs, it becomes necessary to encourage internal political conflict and/or infiltrate the government.

5) No one nation can be permitted to gain military dominance, because this would lead to a lack of conflict for power, and may lead to peace!

P.S. owners of the Federal Reserve:

1) Rothschild Banks of London and Berlin

2) Lazard Brothers Bank of Paris

3) Israel Moses Sieff Bank of Italy

4) Warburg Batiks of Hamburg and Amsterdam

5) Lehman Brothers Bank of New York

6) Kuhn Loeb Bank of New York

7) Chase Manhattan Bank of New York (controlled by the Rockefellers)

8 Goldman Sachs Bank of New York

Re: Who are the members of the New World Oder
« Reply #3 on: February 27, 2008, 12:59:18 PM »

PRESIDENT CFR MEMBERSHIP LIST
George W. Bush
Bill Clinton
George H.W. Bush
Jimmy Carter
Gerald Ford
Richard Nixon
Dwight Eisenhower
Herbert Hoover
Dick Cheney (Vice-President)
Al Gore (Vice-President)

US GOVERNMENT
Warren Christopher
Robert Blackwill, Nat. Security Council – CFR
Membership List, B
Lee Aspin (Deceased)
Frank H. T. Rhodes, Bd. Of Directors -- CFR
James B. Holderman, Bd. Of Directors -- CFR
D. Allen Bromley, Bd. Of Directors -- CFR
Colin L. Powell
Lori Murray, Arms Cont. & Disarm. Agency -- CFR
Lawrence Scheinman, Arms Cont. & Disarm.
Agency -- CFR
Bruce Babbitt
Henry Cisneros
George Stephanopoulos, Director, Communications
-- CFR

Willian J. Crowe, Chief Foreign Intelligence Advisory Bd. -- CFR

Nancy Soderberg, Staff Director, National Secuity Council -- CFR

Samuel R. Berger, Deputy Advisor, National Security -- CFR

W. Bowman Cutter, Deputy Assistant, National Economic Council -- CFR

Donna Shalala

Alice Rivlin, Deputy Director -- CFR

Roger Altman

Michael Nacht, Arms Cont. & Disarm. Agency -- CFR

William R. Graham, Jr., Science Advisor to President & Director -- CFR

Seth Hurwitz, White House, Advisory Committee -- CFR

Robert R. Glauber

James H. Billington, Librarian, Chmn. Trust Fund Board -- CFR

Ruth Ann Stewart, Asst. Librarian National Programs -- CFR

David C. Mulford

Mark Penn

Thomas Graham, Jr., General Council -- CFR Membership List

William Schneier, Chmn., General Advisory Council -- CFR

Richard Burt, Negotiator On Strategic Defense Arms -- CFR

David Smith, Negotiator, Defense & Space -- CFR

Robert M. Bestani

Condoleezza Rice
J. French Hill
John M. Niehuss

DEPARTMENT OF STATE CFR MEMBERSHIP LIST

Strobe Talbott (Special Advisor For CIS) -- CFR Membership List
Thomas R. Pickering (Russia) -- CFR
Morton I. Abramowitz (Turkey) -- CFR
Michael H. Armacost (Japan) -- CFR
Shirly Temple Black (Czechoslovakia) -- CFR Membership List
Julia Chang Bloch (Nepal) -- CFR
Henry E. Catto, Jr. (Great Britain) -- CFR
Frances Cook (Camaroon) -- CFR
Edward P. Djerejian (Syria) -- CFR
Geoge E. Moose (Senegal) -- CFR
John D. Negroponte (Mexico) -- CFR Membership List
Edward N. Ney (Canada) -- CFR
Robert B. Oakley (Pakistan) -- CFR
Robert H. Pelletreau, Jr. (Tunisia) -- CFR
Christopher H. Phillips (Brunei) -- CFR
Nicholas Platt (Phillipines) -- CFR
James W. Spain (Maldives & Sri Lanka) -- CFR
Terence A. Todman (Argentina) -- CFR
Frank G. Wisner II (Egypt) -- CFR
Warren Zimmerman (Yugoslavia) -- CFR
Madeleine Albright, UN Amabassador -- CFR
Clifton Wharton, Jr., Deputy Sec. -- CFR

Lynn Davis, Under Sec. for International Security Affairs -- CFR, TC

Brandon H. Grove, Dir. of Foreign Service Institute -- CFR Membership List

H. Allen Holms, Asst. Sec., Bureau Of Politico-Military Affairs -- CFR

John H. Kelly, Asst. Sec., Near East-South Asian Affairs -- CFR

Alexander F. Watson, Deputy Rep., United Nations -- CFR

Jonathan Moore, UN Mission -- CFR

Joseph Verner Reed, Chief of Protocol -- CFR

Dennis B. Ross, Director, Policy Planning Staff -- CFR

Edward Perkins, Dir. of Personnel -- CFR

Abraham David Sofaer, Legal Advisor -- CFR

Peter Tanoff, Under Sec. for Political Affairs -- CFR, TC

Brian Atwood, Under Sec. For Management -- CFR

Joan E. Spero, Under Sec. Eco. & Ag. Affairs -- CFR

George E. Moose, Asst. Sec. African Affairs -- CFR

Winston Lord, Asst. Sec., East Asian & Pacific Affairs -- CFR, TC

Stephen A. Oxman, Asst. Sec., European Affairs -- CFR

Timothy E. Wirth, Counselor – CFR

UNITED STATES CONGRESS CFR MEMBERSHIP LIST

Howard L. Berman (D-CA) -- CFR Membership List

Thomas S. Foley (D-WA) -- CFR

Sam Gejdenson (D-CT) -- CFR

Richard A. Gephardt (D-MO) -- CFR

Newton L. Gingrich (R-GA) -- CFR

Lee H. Hamilton (D-IN) -- TC

Amory Houghton, Jr. (R-NY) -- CFR

Nancy Lee Johnson (R-CT) -- CFR

Jim Leach (R-IA) -- TC

John Lewis (D-GA) -- CFR

Robert T. Matsui (D-CA) -- CFR

Dave K. Mccurdy (D-OK) -- CFR

Eleanor Homes Norton (D-DC) -- CFR Membership List

Thomas El Petri (R-WI) -- CFR

Charles B. Rangel (D-NY) -- TC

Carlos A. Romero-Barcelo (D-PR) -- CFR

Patricia Schroeder (D-CO) -- CFR

Peter Smith (R-VT) -- CFR

Olympia J. Snow (R-ME) -- CFR

John M. Spratt (D-SC) -- CFR

Louis Stokes (D-OH) – CFR

David L. Boren (D-OK) -- CFR

William Bradley (D-NJ) -- CFR

John H. Chafee (R-RI) -- CFR, TC

William S. Cohen (R-ME) -- CFR, TC

Christopher J. Dodd (D-CT) -- CFR

Dianne Feinstein (D-CA) -- TC

Bob Graham (D-FL) -- CFR

Joseph I. Lieberman (D-CT) -- CFR Membership List

George J. MiTChell (D-ME) -- CFR

Claiborne Pell (D-RI) -- CFR

Larry Pressler (R-SD) -- CFR

Charles S. Robb (D-VA) -- CFR, TC

John D. Rockefeller, IV (D-WV) -- CFR, TC

William Roth, Jr. (R-DE) -- CFR, TC

JUDICIARY CFR MEMBERSHIP LIST

Sandra Day O'Connor, Assoc. Justice, U.S. Supreme Court -- CFR Membership List

Steve G. Breyer, Chief Judge, U.S. Court of Appeals, First Circuit, Boston -- CFR

Ruth B. Ginsburg, U.S. Court Of Appeals, Wash., DC Circuit -- CFR

Laurence H. Silberman, U.S. Court of Appeals, Wash., DC Circuit – CFR

BANKING CFR MEMBERSHIP LIST

Chase Manhattan Corp.:

Thomas G. Labrecque, Chairman & CEO – CFR Membership List, TC

Robert R. Douglass, Vice Chairman -- CFR Membership List

Willard C. BuTCher, Dir. -- CFR

Richard W. Lyman, Dir. -- CFR

Joan Ganz Cooney, Dir. -- CFR

David T. Mclaughlin, Dir. -- CFR

Edmund T. Pratt, Jr., Dir. -- CFR

Henry B. Schacht, Dir. -- CFR
Chemical Bank:
Walter V. Shipley, Chairman -- CFR
Robert J. Callander, President -- CFR
William C. Pierce, Executive Officer -- CFR
Randolph W. Bromery, Dir. -- CFR
Charles W. Duncan, Jr., Dir. -- CFR
George V. Grune, Dir. -- CFR
Helen L. Kaplan, Dir. -- CFR
Lawrence G. Rawl, Dir. -- CFR
Michael I. Sovern, Dir. -- CFR
Richard D. Wood, Dir. -- CFR
Citicorp:
John S. Reed. Chairman -- CFR
William R. Rhodes, Vice Chairman -- CFR
Richard S. Braddock, President -- CFR
John M. DeuTCh, Dir. -- CFR
Clifton C. Garvin, Jr., Dir -- CFR
C. Peter Mccolough, Dir. -- CFR
Rozanne L. Ridgeway, Dir. -- CFR
Franklin A. Thomas, Dir. -- CFR
First City Bancorp, Texas:
A. Robert Abboud, CEO -- CFR
Morgan Guaranty:
Lewis T. Preston, Chairman -- CFR
Bankers Trust New York Corporation:
Charles S. Stanford, Jr., Chairman -- CFR
Alfred Brittain III, Dir. -- CFR
Vernon E. Jordan, Jr., Dir -- CFR
Richard L. Gelb, Dir. -- CFR
Patricia Carry Stewart, Dir. -- CFR
First National Bank of Chicago:

Barry F. Sullivan -- TC
Manufacturers Hanover Directors:
Cyrus Vance -- CFR
G. Robert Durham -- CFR
George B. Munroe -- CFR
Marina V. N. Whitman -- CFR, TC
Charles J. Pilliod, Jr. -- CFR
Bank America:
Andrew F. Brimmer, Dir. -- CFR
Ignazio E. Lozano, Jr., Dir. -- CFR
Ruben F. Mettler, Dir. -- CFR
Securities & Exchange Commission:
Michael D. Mann, Dir. International Affairs -- CFR

FEDERAL RESERVE CFR MEMBERSHIP LIST

Alan Greenspan, ChairmaN – CFR Membership List, TC
E. Gerald Corrigan, V. Chmn./Pres. NY Fed. Res. Bank -- CFR
Richard N. Cooper, Chmn. Boston Fed. Res. Bank -- CFR
Sam Y. Cross, Manager, Foreign Open Market Acct. -- CFR
Robert F. Erburu, Chmn. San Francisco Fed. Res. Bank -- CFR
Robert P. Forrestal, Pres. Atlanta Fed. Res. Bank -- CFR
Bobby R. Inman, Chmn., Dallas Fed. Res. Bank -- CFR, TC
Robert H. Knight, Esq. -- CFR
Steven Muller -- CFR

John R. Opel -- CFR
Anthony M. Solomon -- CFR, TC
Edwin M. Truman, Staff Dir. International Finance -- CFR
Cyrus R. Vance -- CFR
Paul Volcker -- CFR, TC
MEDIA CFR MEMBERSHIP LIST
CBS:
Laurence A. Tisch, CEO -- CFR Membership List
Roswell Gilpatric -- CFR
James Houghton -- CFR, TC
Henry Schacht -- CFR, TC
Dan Rather -- CFR
Richard Hottelet -- CFR
Frank Stanton -- CFR
NBC/RCA:
John F. Welch, CEO -- CFR
Jane Pfeiffer -- CFR
Lester Crystal -- CFR, TC
R.W. Sonnenfeidt -- CFR, TC
John Petty -- CFR
David Brinkley -- CFR
John Chancellor -- CFR
Marvin Kalb -- CFR
Irving R. Levine -- CFR
Herbert Schlosser -- CFR
Peter G. Peterson -- CFR
John Sawhill -- CFR
ABC:
Thomas S. Murphy, CEO -- CFR
Barbara Walters -- CFR
John Connor -- CFR

Diane Sawyer -- CFR
John Scall -- CFR
Public Broadcast Service:
Robert Mcneil -- CFR
Jim Lehrer -- CFR
C. Hunter-Gault -- CFR
Hodding Carter III -- CFR
Daniel Schorr -- CFR
Associated Press:
Stanley Swinton -- CFR
Harold Anderson -- CFR
Katharine Graham -- CFR, TC
Reuters:
Michael Posner -- CFR
Baltimore Sun:
Henry Trewhitt -- CFR
Washington Times:
Arnaud De Borchgrave -- CFR
Children's TV Workshop (Sesame Street):
Joan Ganz Cooney, Pres. -- CFR
Cable News Network:
W. Thomas Johnson, Pres. -- TC
Daniel Schorr -- CFR
U.S. News & World Report:
David Gergen -- TC
New York Times Co.:
Richard Gelb -- CFR
William Scranton -- CFR, TC
John F. Akers, Dir. -- CFR
Louis V. Gerstner, Jr., Dir. -- CFR
George B. Munroe, Dir. -- CFR
Donald M. Stewart, Dir. -- CFR

Cyrus R. Vance, Dir. -- CFR
A.M. Rosenthal -- CFR
Seymour Topping -- CFR
James Greenfield -- CFR
Max Frankel -- CFR
Jack Rosenthal -- CFR
John Oakes -- CFR
Harrison Salisbury -- CFR
H.L. Smith -- CFR
Steven Rattner -- CFR
Richard Burt -- CFR
Flora Lewis -- CFR
Time, Inc.:
Ralph Davidson -- CFR
Donal M. Wilson -- CFR
Henry Grunwald -- CFR
Alexander Heard -- CFR
Sol Linowitz -- CFR
Thomas Watson, Jr. -- CFR
Strobe Talbott -- CFR
Newsweek/Washington Post:
Katharine Graham -- CFR
N. Deb. Katzenbach -- CFR
Robert Christopher -- CFR
Osborne Elliot -- CFR
Phillip Geyelin -- CFR
Murry Marder -- CFR
Maynard Parker -- CFR
George Will -- CFR, TC
Robert Kaiser -- CFR
Meg Greenfield -- CFR
Walter Pincus -- CFR

Murray Gart -- CFR
Peter Osnos -- CFR
Don Oberdorfer -- CFR
Dow Jones & Co (Wall Street Journal):
Richard Wood -- CFR
Robert Bartley -- CFR, TC
Karen House -- CFR

National Review:
Wm. F. Buckley, Jr. -- CFR
Readers Digest:
George V. Grune, CEO -- CFR
William G. Bowen, Dir. -- CFR
Syndicated Columnists
Geogia Anne Geyer -- CFR
Ben J. Wattenberg – CFR

US MILITARY CFR MEMBERSHIP LIST
Department Of Defense:
Les Aspin, Secretary of Defense -- CFR
Membership List
Frank G. WisnerII, Under Secretary for Policy -- CFR
Henry S. Rowen, Asst. Sec., International Security Affairs -- CFR
Judy Ann Miller, Dep. Asst. Sec. Nuclear Forces & Arms Control -- CFR
W. Bruce Weinrod, Dep. Asst. Sec., Europe & NATO -- CFR
Adm. Seymour Weiss, Chairman, Defense Policy Board -- CFR

Charles M. Herzfeld, Dir. Defense Research & Engineering -- CFR
Andrew W. Marshall, Dir., Net Assessment -- CFR
Michael P. W. Stone, Secretary of the Army -- CFR
Donald B. Rice, Secretary of the Air Force -- CFR
Franklin C. Miller, Dep. Asst. Sec. Nuclear Forces & Arms Control -- CFR

Allied Supreme Commanders:
1949-52 Eisenhower -- CFR Membership List
1952-53 Ridgeway -- CFR
1953-56 Gruenther -- CFR
1956-63 Norstad -- CFR
1963-69 Lemnitzer -- CFR
1969-74 Goodpaster -- CFR
1974-79 Haig -- CFR
1979-87 Rogers -- CFR, TC
Superintendents of the U.S. Military Academy at West Point:
1960-63 Westmoreland -- CFR Membership List
1963-66 Lampert -- CFR
1966-68 Bennett -- CFR
1970-74 Knowlton -- CFR
1974-77 Berry -- CFR
1977-81 Goodpaster -- CFR
CFR Military Fellows, 1991:
Col. William M. Drennan, Jr., USAF -- CFR
Col. Wallace C. Gregson, USMC -- CFR
Col. Jack B. Wood, USA -- CFR
CFR Military Fellows, 1992:
Col. David M. Mize, USMC -- CFR Membership List
Col. John P. Rose, USA -- CFR

Joint Chiefs of Staff:

Gen. Colin L. Powell, Chairman -- CFR

Gen. Carl E. Vuono, Army -- CFR

Gen. John T. Chain, Co Sac -- CFR

Gen. Merril A. Mcpeak, Co Pac AF -- CFR

Lt. Gen. George L. Butler, Dir. Strategic Plans & Policy -- CFR

Lt. Gen. Charles T. Boyd, Com. Air Univ. -- CFR

Lt. Gen. Bradley C. Hosmer, AF Inspector General -- CFR

Secretaries of Defense:

1957-59 Mcelroy -- CFR Membership List

1959-61 Gates -- CFR

1961-68 McNamara -- CFR, TC

1969-73 Laird -- CFR

1973-75 Richardson -- CFR, TC

1975-77 Rumsfeld -- CFR

1977-80 Brown -- CFR, TC

1980-88 Weinberger -- CFR, TC

1988- Carlucci -- CFR

1988- Cheney -- CFR

Additional Military:

Mg R.C. Bowman -- CFR Membership List

Bg F. Brown -- CFR

Lt Col W. Clark -- CFR

Adm Wm. Crowe -- CFR

Col P. M. Dawkins -- CFR

V. Adm. Thor Hanson -- CFR

Col W. Hauser -- CFR

Maj R. Kimmitt -- CFR

Gen W. Knowlton -- CFR

V. Adm J. Lee -- CFR

Col D. Mead -- CFR
Mg Jack Merritt -- CFR
Gen E. Meyer -- CFR
Col Wm. E. Odom -- CFR
Col L. Olvey -- CFR
Col Geo. K. Osborn -- CFR
Mg J. Pustay -- CFR
Lg E.L. Rowny -- CFR
Capt Gary Sick -- CFR
Mg De Witt Smith -- CFR
Bg Perry Smith -- CFR
Ltg Wm. Y. Smith -- CFR
Col W. Taylor -- CFR
Adm S. Turner -- CFR
Mg J. Welch -- CFR
Gen J. Wickham – CFR

BUSINESS CFR MEMBERSHIP LIST

Exxon Corporation
Lawrence G. Rawl, Chairman -- CFR Membership List
Lee R. Raymond, President -- CFR, TC
Jack G. Clarke, Sr., Vice President -- CFR
Randolph W. Bromery, Dir. -- CFR
D. Wayne Calloway, Dir. -- CFR
Texaco
Alfred C. Decrane,Jr., Chairman -- CFR Membership List
John Brademas, Dir. -- CFR, TC
Willard C. BuTCher, Dir. -- CFR
William J. Crowe, Jr., Dir. -- CFR, TC

John K. Mckinley, Dir. -- CFR
Thomas S. Murphy, Dir. -- CFR
Atlantic Richfield-Arco:
Hannah H. Gray, Dir. -- CFR
Donal M. Kendall,Dir. -- CFR, TC
Henry Wendt, Dir. -- TC
Shell Oil Co.:
Frank H. Richardson, CEO -- CFR Membership List
Rand V. Araskog, Dir. -- CFR, TC
Mobil Corp.:
Allan E. Murray, Chairman & President – CFR
Membership List, TC
Lewis M. Branscomb, Dir. -- CFR
Samuel C. Johnson, Dir. -- TC
Helene L. Kaplan, Dir. -- CFR
Charles S. Sanford, Jr., Dir. -- CFR
Tenneco, Inc.:
James L. Ketelsen, Chairman -- CFR
W. Michael Blumenthal, Dir. -- CFR
Joseph J. Sisco, Dir. – CFR
General Motors Corp.:
Marina V.N. Whitman, VP – CFR Membership List,
TC
Anne L. Armstrong, Dir. -- CFR
Marvin L. Goldberger, Dir. -- CFR
Edmund T. Pratt, Jr., Dir. -- CFR
Dennis Weatherstone, Dir. -- CFR
Leon H. Sullivan, Dir. -- CFR
Thomas H. Wyman, Dir. -- CFR
Ford Motor Company:
Clifton R. Wharton, Dir. -- CFR
Roberto C. Goizueta, Dir. -- CFR

GE/NBC Corp.:
John F. Welch, Jr. Chairman -- CFR Membership List
David C. Jones -- CFR
Lewis T. Preston -- CFR
Frank H.T. Rhodes -- CFR
Walter B. Wriston -- CFR
Deere & Co:
Hans W. Becherer, Chairman/CEO -- CFR
IBM:
John F. Akers, Chairman -- CFR Membership List
C. Michael Armstrong, Sr. VP -- CFR
Amtrak:
William S. Norman, Executive VP -- CFR
AT&T:
Robert E. Allen, Chairman & CEO -- CFR Membership List
Randall L. Tobias, Vice Chairman -- CFR
Louis V. Gerstner, Dir. -- CFR
Juanita M. Kreps, Dir. -- CFR
Donald F. Mchenry, Dir. -- CFR
Henry B. Schacht, Dir. -- CFR
Michael I. Sovern, Dir. -- CFR
Franklin A. Thamas, Dir. -- CFR
Rawleigh Warner, Jr., Dir. -- CFR
Thomas H. Wyman, Dir. -- CFR
Chrysler Corp.:
Joseph A. Califano, Jr., Dir. -- CFR Membership List
Peter A. Magowan, Dir. -- CFR
American Express Co.:
James D. Robinson,Ceo -- CFR Membership List
Joan Edelman Spero -- TC

Anne L. Armstrong -- CFR

William G. Bowen -- CFR

Charles W. Duncan, Jr. -- CFR

Richard M. Furlaud -- CFR

Vernon E. Jordan, Jr. -- CFR, TC

Henry A. Kissinger -- CFR, TC

Frank P. Popoff -- CFR

Robert V. Roosa -- CFR

Joseph H. Williams – CFR

Richard D. Wood, CEO, Eli Lily & Co -- CFR

Richard M. Furlaud, CEO, Bristol-Myers Squibb Co -- CFR

Frank Peter Popoff, CEO, Dow Chemical Co. -- CFR

Charles Peter McColough, Chmn Ex. Comm, Xerox -- CFR

Rozanne L. Ridgewar, Dir., 3M, RJR Nabisco, Union Carbide -- CFR

Ruben F. Mettler, Former CEO, TRW, Inc. -- CFR

Henry B. Schacht, CEO, Cummins Engines -- CFR

Edmund T. Pratt, Jr., CEO, Pfizer, Inc. -- CFR

Rand V. Araskog, CEO, ITT Corp. -- CFR, TC

W. Michael Blumenthal, Chairman, Unisys Corp. -- CFR

Joseph John Sisco, Dir., Geico, Raytheon, Gillette -- CFR

J.Fred Bucy, Former Pres, CEO, Texas Instruments -- CFR

Paul A. Allaire, Chairman, CEO, Xerox Corp. -- TC

Dwayne O. Andreas, Chairman, CEO, Archer Midland Daniels -- TC

James E. Burke, Chairman, CEO Em., Johnson & Johnson -- TC

D. Wayne Calloway, Chairman, CEO, Pepsico -- TC

Frank C. Carlucci, Vice Chmn., The Carlyle Group -- TC

Lynn E. Davis, VP, Dir., Rand Corp -- TC

Stephen Friedman, Sr., VP, Co-Chairman, Goldman, Sachs -- TC

Louis V. Gerstner, Jr., Chairman, CEO, RJR Nabisco -- TC

Joseph T. Gorman, Chairman, Pres, CEO, TRW Inc. -- TC

Maurice R. Greenberg, Chairman, CEO, American International Group -- TC

Robert D. Hass, Chairman, CEO, Levi Strauss -- TC

David J. Hennigar, Chairman, Crownx, Vice Chairman, Crown Life -- TC

Robert D. Hormats, Vice Chairman, Goldman Sachs Int. -- TC

James R. Houghton, Chairman, CEO, Corning Inc. -- TC

Donald R. Keough, President, CEO, The Coca Cola Co. -- TC

Henry A. Kissinger, Chairman, Kissinger Assoc. -- TC

Whitney Macmillan, Chairman, CEO, Cargill, Inc. -- TC

Robert S. McNamara, Former President, The World Bank -- TC

William D. Ruckershaus, Chairman, CEO, Browning-Ferris Ind. -- TC

David Stockman, Gen Partner, The Blackstone Group -- CFR

Henry Wendt, Chmn, Smith Kline Beecham – TC

EDUCATION CFR MEMBERSHIP LIST

University Professors:

Graham Allison, Prof. Of Gov., Harvard Univ. -- TC

Zbigniew Brzezinski, Prof., Johns Hopkins -- TC

Gerald L. Curtis, Prof. Poli Sci, Columbia Univ. -- TC

Martin S. Feldstein, Prof. Econ, Harvard Univ. -- TC

Richard N. Gardner, Prof. Law, Columbia Univ. -- TC

Joseph S. Nye, Jr., Prof. Int'l Affairs, Harvard Univ. -- TC

Robert D. Putnam, Prof. Politics, Havard Univ. -- TC

Henry Rosovsky, Prof. Harvard Univ. -- TC

Geoge P. Shultz, Hon. Fellow, Stanford Univ. -- TC

Lester C. Thorow, Dean, Sloan School if Mgmt., MIT -- TC

Paul Volcker, Prof. Int'l Econ., Princeton Univ -- TC

College & University Presidents:

Robert H. Edwards, Bowdoin College -- CFR

Vartan Gregorian, Brown University -- CFR

Hanna Holbom Gray, University of Chicago -- CFR

Joseph S. Murphy, City Univ. of NY -- CFR

Michael I. Sovern, Columbia Univ. -- CFR

Andrew J. Nathan, Columbia Univ. -- CFR

Everette Dennis, Jr., Columbia Univ. -- CFR

Harriet Zuckerman, Columbia Univ. -- CFR

Frank H.T. Rhodes, Cornell University -- CFR

Kurt Gottfried, Cornell University – CFR
Carl Edward Sagan, Cornell University -- CFR
James T. Laney, Emory University -- CFR
Rev. Joseph A. O'Hare, Fordham Univ. -- CFR
Thomas Ehrlich, Indiana Univ. -- CFR
Steven Muller, Johns Hopkins Univ. -- CFR
Alice S. Iichman, Sarah Lawrence College -- CFR
Edward T. Foote, II, University Of Miami -- CFR
S. Frederick Starr, Oberlin College -- CFR, TC
Joseph Duffey, Chans., Univ. Of Mass. -- CFR
John M. DeuTCh, Institute Professor, MIT -- CFR, TC
Lester C. Thurow, Dean, Sloan Sch., MIT -- CFR
Bernard Harleston, City College of NY -- CFR
John Brademus, New York University -- CFR, TC
Wesley W. Posvar, University of Pittsburg -- CFR
Harold T. Shapiro, Princeton University -- CFR
Charles W. Duncan, Jr., Chmn, Rice University -- CFR
Dennis O'Brien, Univ. Of Rochester -- CFR
David Baltimore, Rockefeller University -- CFR
Donald Dennedy, Stanford University -- CFR
Richard Wall Lyman, Pres. Em., Stanford -- CFR
Hans M. Mark, Chancellor, Univ. of Texas -- CFR
Robert H. Donaldson, Univ. of Tulsa -- CFR
Stephen J. Trachtenberg, George Washington Univ. -- CFR
William H. Danforth, Washington University, St. Louis -- CFR
John D. Wilson, Washington & Lee University -- CFR
Nannerl O. Keohane, Wellesley University – CFR

Madeleine K. Albright, Principal, The Albright Group LLC, Washington, DC; former U.S. Secretary of State

Graham Allison, Director, Belfer Center for Science and International Affairs, Harvard University, Cambridge, MA

G. Allen Andreas, Chairman and Chief Executive, Archer Daniels Midland Company, Decatur, IL

Michael H. Armacost, Shorenstein Distinguished Fellow, Asia/Pacific Research Center, Stanford University, Hillsborough, CA; former President, The Brookings Institution; former U.S. Ambassador to Japan; former U.S. Under Secretary of State for Political Affairs

Charlene Barshefsky, Senior International Partner, Wilmer, Cutler & Pickering, Washington, DC; former U.S. Trade Representative

Alan R. Batkin, Vice Chairman, Kissinger Associates, New York, NY

Doug Bereuter, President, The Asia Foundation, San Francisco, CA; former Member, U.S. House of Representatives

*C. Fred Bergsten, Director, Institute for International Economics, Washington, DC; former U.S. Assistant Secretary of the Treasury for International Affairs

Catherine Bertini, Professor of Public Administration, Maxwell School of Citizenship and Public Affairs, Syracuse University, Syracuse, NY; former Under-Secretary-General for Management, United Nations

Dennis C. Blair, USN (Ret.), President and Chief Executive Officer, Institute for Defense Analyses, Alexandria, VA; former Commander in Chief, U.S. Pacific Command

Herminio Blanco Mendoza, Private Office of Herminio Blanco, Mexico City, NL; former Mexican Secretary of Commerce and Industrial Development

Geoffrey T. Boisi, Chairman & Senior Partner, Roundtable Investment Partners LLC, New York, NY; former Vice Chairman, JPMorgan Chase, New York, NY

Stephen W. Bosworth, Dean, Fletcher School of Law and Diplomacy, Tufts University, Medford, MA; former U.S. Ambassador to the Republic of Korea

David G. Bradley, Chairman, Atlantic Media Company, Washington, DC

Harold Brown, Counselor, Center for Strategic and International Studies, Washington, DC; General Partner, Warburg Pincus & Company, New York, NY; former U.S. Secretary of Defense

*Zbigniew Brzezinski, Counselor, Center for Strategic and International Studies, Washington, DC; Robert Osgood Professor of American Foreign Affairs, Paul Nitze School of Advanced International Studies, Johns Hopkins University; former U.S. Assistant to the President for National Security Affairs

Quotes:

In the mainline media, those who adhere to the position that there is some kind of "conspiracy" pushing us towards a world government are virulently ridiculed. The standard attack maintains that the so-called "New World Order" is the product of turn-of-the-century, right-wing, bigoted, anti-semitic racists acting in the tradition of the long-debunked Protocols of the Learned Elders of Zion, now promulgated by some Militias and other right-wing hate groups.

The historical record does not support that position to any large degree but it has become the mantra of the socialist left and their cronies, the media.

The term "New World Order" has been used thousands of times in this century by proponents in high places of federalized world government. Some of those involved in this collaboration to achieve world order have been Jewish. The preponderance are not, so it most definitely is not a Jewish agenda. For years, leaders in education, industry, the media, banking, etc., have promoted those with the same Weltanschauung (world view) as theirs. Of course, someone might say that just because individuals promote their friends doesn't constitute a conspiracy. That's true in the usual sense. However, it does represent an "open conspiracy," as described by noted Fabian Socialist H.G. Wells in The Open Conspiracy: Blue Prints for a World Revolution (1928).

In 1913, prior to the passage of the Federal Reserve Act President Wilson's The New Freedom was published, in which he revealed:
"Since I entered politics, I have chiefly had men's views confided to me privately. Some of the biggest men in the U. S., in the field of commerce and manufacturing, are afraid of somebody, are afraid of something. They know that there is a power somewhere so organized, so subtle, so watchful, so interlocked, so complete, so pervasive, that they had better not speak above their breath when they speak in condemnation of it."

On November 21, 1933, President Franklin Roosevelt wrote a letter to Col. Edward Mandell House, President Woodrow Wilson's close advisor:
"The real truth of the matter is, as you and I know, that a financial element in the larger centers has owned the Government ever since the days of Andrew Jackson... "
That there is such a thing as a cabal of power brokers who control government behind the scenes has been detailed several times in this century by credible sources. Professor Carroll Quigley was Bill Clinton's mentor at Georgetown University. President Clinton has publicly paid homage to the influence Professor Quigley had on his life. In Quigley's magnum opus Tragedy and Hope (1966), he states:

"There does exist and has existed for a generation, an international ... network which operates, to some extent, in the way the radical right believes the Communists act. In fact, this network, which we may identify as the Round Table Groups, has no aversion to cooperating with the Communists, or any other groups and frequently does so. I know of the operations of this network because I have studied it for twenty years and was permitted for two years, in the early 1960s, to examine its papers and secret records. I have no aversion to it or to most of its aims and have, for much of my life, been close to it and to many of its instruments. I have objected, both in the past and recently, to a few of its policies... but in general my chief difference of opinion is that it wishes to remain unknown, and I believe its role in history is significant enough to be known."

Even talk show host Rush Limbaugh, an outspoken critic of anyone claiming a push for global government, said on his February 7, 1995 program: "You see, if you amount to anything in Washington these days, it is because you have been plucked or handpicked from an Ivy League school -- Harvard, Yale, Kennedy School of Government -- you've shown an aptitude to be a good Ivy League type, and so you're plucked so-to-speak, and you are assigned success. You are assigned a certain role in government somewhere, and then your success is monitored and tracked, and you go where the pluckers and the handpickers can put you."

On May 4, 1993, Council on Foreign Relations (CFR) president Leslie Gelb said on The Charlie Rose Show that:

"... you [Charlie Rose] had me on [before] to talk about the New World Order! I talk about it all the time. It's one world now. The Council [CFR] can find, nurture, and begin to put people in the kinds of jobs this country needs. And that's going to be one of the major enterprises of the Council under me."

President Bill Clinton

Bilderbergers Planned Kosovo War in 1996

During and following the 1996 Bilderberg Conference, we asserted that Bilderberger Bill

Clinton would be re-elected as U.S. president; that he would promptly break his promise to bring American troops home from Bosnia, but that he would re-position them in Hungary and the surrounding countries instead and pass command of the Bosnian operation to a German general and 3,000 German combat troops from Heidelberg [this later occurred, in October, 1996]; and that the Bilderbergers had thereafter arranged to inflame the Serbs by pursuing the war criminals in their midst for trial before a new International Court [the Serbs, a proud but experienced people, side-stepped this provocation by persuading the lower- and middle-level suspects to voluntarily surrender].

If that failed to incite a Balkan war, then we pointed out that they were prepared to utilize Kosovo to bring one about:

"When war comes, as expected, Kosovo, at the southern tip of the Serbian Republic, may be the flashpoint that ignites a wider war involving Greece, Albania, Bulgaria, Russia, and Turkey - in addition to the hapless U.S. and NATO troops caught in the middle. Kosovo, "the Jerusalem of the Balkans", is a self-proclaimed nominally independent "republic", presided over by "President" Ibrahim Rugova. It is, in fact, a province of Serbia, though its population is largely of Albanian descent. The United States, though on record as recommending more "autonomy" for Kosovo, treats the province to all intents and purposes as a de facto independent state, a fact which infuriates the Serbians. Twice -

once in 1992 and again in 1993 - Presidents of the United States have threatened Serbian President Slobodan Milosevic with military retribution "in the event of a conflict in Kosovo caused by Serbian action." To add insult to injury, the U.S. now plans to establish an "official presence" in "the capital of Kosovo." Aggrieved by this, and rightly sensing the intent of the United States to encircle and contain them, the Serbians are likely to appeal to an increasingly-nationalistic Russia, their traditional protectors, for help and military assistance. As reported by Germany's DIE ZEIT, "Serbia is every place where there are Serbian trenches or Serbian graves", according to Serbian opposition leader Val Draskovic. That means that Serbia will fight to retain Kovoso, in spite of the fact that its population is 90% Albanian. The Albanian Kosovans, determined to be independent, will fight back. That will likely draw into the conflict the 3.4 million inhabitants of Albania proper, together with the Albanians of Montenegro and Macedonia. Albania also has openly-expressed designs on Macedonia's western provinces, largely populated by Albanians: at least one armed insurrection directed by Albania has been foiled by the Macedonian authorities, and the Albanians continue to openly support and encourage Macedonian Albanian separatist groups. Bulgaria, which considers Macedonians to be "western Bulgarians", may then go to war for the fourth time this century to seize the opportunity to finally settle its territorial claim there. Greece, already incensed by Macedonia's use of the Greek

"Verging Sun" symbol on its flag and suspicious of the Macedonian Republic's supposed intention to form a "Greater Macedonia" by inciting insurrection and separation in the Greek province of Macedonia, may well then take advantage of events to settle the issue once and for all. Turkey, acting in defense of its Muslim brethren in Bosnia, and infuriated by the actions of its traditional rival Greece against the Macedonian Republic, could then scarcely be refrained from joining the fray.

The "Albanian issue", centered in Kosovo and overshadowed by the larger Serb-Bosnian tensions, is a powder keg waiting to explode. And when it does, the whole region will explode with it." - from our 1996 BILDERBERGER REPORT [almost three years later, these things are now happening!]

The Serbs, scenting the trap thus laid for them, have confined themselves to short, repressive police actions against the Kosovan Albanian population, none of which have been sufficient in duration, extent or intensity to provide the pretext necessary for the Bilderberger elite to rally Western European and American public support for a full-fledged military engagement of the Serbs. So their methodical preparation, financing and arming of the newly-revealed Kosovan Liberation Army has so far provided the Bilderbergers with no dividends at all...and the clock is running on their schedule. They need this war, and they need it soon.

Hans F. Sennholz, an economist who studied under the legendary free-market libertarian Ludwig von Mises, explained the government's accounting gimmick like this:

Imagine a corporation suffering losses and being deep in debt. In order to boost its stock price and the bonuses of its officers, the corporation quietly borrows funds in the bond market and uses them not only to cover its losses but also to retire some corporate stock and thereby bid up its price. And imagine the management boasting of profits and surpluses. But that's what the Clinton Administration has been doing with alacrity and brazenness. It suffers sizable budget deficits, increasing the national debt by hundreds of billions of dollars, but uses trust funds to meet expenditures and then boasts of surpluses which excites the spending predilection of politicians in both parties.

(Broke, by Glenn Beck & Kevin Balfe)

President George Bush

The New World Order

As the 20th-century idols of <u>atheism</u>, <u>humanism</u> and <u>communism</u> are falling worldwide a spiritual vacuum is left that must be filled. In the resulting contest for the souls and minds of Americans in this new world order, the Church faces formidable opponents in godless liberal collectivists, neo-conservative fascists, globalists, New Age religion, Islam and Satanism.

No longer are we only threatened from without by a group of balding hard-line Communists - we are now threatened from within - by a group of intelligent, well-dressed globalists who are convincing America and the nations of the world that the only way to lasting world peace is the establishment of a ... "New World Order."

New World Order is a term used to describe the uniting of the world's superpowers to secure and maintain global peace, safety, and security. Synonymous with the term New World Order are the terms one world government, global governance, and globalization. All these terms are used interchangeably and at different times to communicate to different audiences. Make no mistake - they all basically mean the same thing.

"A nation can survive its fools, and even the ambitious. But it cannot survive treason from within. An enemy at the gates is less formidable, for he is known and he carries his banners openly. But the traitor moves among those within the gate freely, his sly whispers rustling through all the alleys, heard in the very halls of government itself. For the traitor appears not traitor, he speaks in the accents familiar to his victims, and he wears their face and their garments, and he appeals to the baseness that lies deep in the hearts of all men. He rots the soul of a nation, he works secretly and unknown in the night to undermine the pillars of a city, he infects the body politic so that it can no longer resist. A murderer is less to be feared." - Cicero, 42 B.C.

Conspiracy Theory or Fact?

While many people dismiss the New World Order as a conspiracy theory, it is neither a conspiracy nor a theory. It may be true there are many conspirators working within the New World Order, in it's broader application, the New World Order is really more of an agenda by a group of international elites that control and manipulate governments, industry and media organizations worldwide. Any intelligent person examining history and events occurring today cannot describe it as a theory either, rather the New World Order is clearly documented in historical documents in both the words and actions of world leaders.

World leaders are excited at the prospects for peace and there has been much talk about entering a "new era" and about the establishment of a "New World Order."

The New World Order agenda is detailed in documents from the Council of Foreign Relations, Trilateral Commission, Bilderberg Group, Club of Rome, United Nations, World Bank, and the International Monetary Fund.

Mikhail Gorbachev was the first world leader to come out publicly with talk of a "new world order," and he did so nearly two years before George Bush caught the vision. In his historic address to the United Nations on December 7, 1988, the Soviet Prime Minister made this dogmatic and even prophetic statement: "Further global progress is now possible only through a quest for universal consensus in the movement towards a new world order."

George Bush proved to be a good and faithful servant of the "brotherhood" in making the "New World Order" agenda a priority focus of his administration. Just before leaving for Helsinki, Finland, early in September 1990 to discuss the Persian Gulf crisis at his summit meeting with Soviet President Gorbachev, President George Bush expressed the hope that "the foundation for the new world order would be laid in Helsinki" and that it would be established under the United Nations.

At the news conference with Gorbachev following their historic meeting, President Bush declared optimistically: "If the nations of the world, acting together, continue as they have been we will set in place the cornerstone of an international order more peaceful than any that we have known."

Then in 1993, the New World Order was established as a legitimate national agenda - by a socialist Democrat, Bill Clinton. Both George Bush and Bill Clinton were beholding to the same secret orders, codes and financiers, and as a result, probably engineered the change of Presidents by manipulating the American people to pull the plug on Bush. George Bush may have actually been running a campaign to LOSE the presidency.

Globalists welcomed this as democracy's finest hour - through manipulation, the democratic system installed a socialist, new age, one-world leader with the charismatic appeal of John F. Kennedy to do their bidding!

During Clinton's reign, New World Order Socialists publicly came out of the closet in the U.S. House of Representatives. The powerful and popular lobby called the Progressive Caucus now began openly espousing the principles of socialism and publicly signed onto the agenda of the Democratic Socialists of America.

Masterfully using the Hegelian Dialectic, Bill Clinton's favorite answer to all questions was government. Got a problem? Bill Clinton's new government program can fix it. Lost your job? Sign up for an employee retraining program. Feeling a little under the weather? A visit to your regional health alliance will shape you up. Having difficulty raising your children? Join our village because "It takes more than a family to raise children."

Bill and Hillary were introducing Americans to the 21st Century "Brave New World" described by Aldous Huxley in 1932 where humanity lives in a carefree, healthy, and technologically advanced society.

Warfare and poverty are to be eliminated in their "village" and everyone is permanently happy due to government-provided conditioning and drugs. Clinton also advanced the more hedonistic society, deriving pleasure from promiscuous sex and drug use, what Huxley called soma - a powerful psychotropic rationed by the government that is taken to escape pain and bad memories through hallucinatory fantasies, referred to as "Holidays". Of course, these things are achieved by eliminating many things that we consider to be central to our identity - family, culture, art, literature, science, religion, and philosophy.

"We are redefining in practical terms the immutable ideals that have guided us from the beginning." - President Bill Clinton

Peace, Safety, and Security
The pacified population accepts it readily enough believing that a world government establishing world peace and preventing a nuclear holocaust could not be considered evil.

While people are saying, "Peace and safety," destruction will come on them suddenly, as labor

pains on a pregnant woman, and they will not escape.
- 1 Thessalonians 5:3

The Price of Security
In a statement to the United Nations Business Council in September 1994, David Rockefeller said, "We are on the verge of a global transformation. All we need is the right major crisis and the nations will accept the new world order."

By the time George W. Bush came into power, the next incremental step necessary to accomplish the global transformation Rockefeller referred to was to convice the American people that it was necessary they abandon the freedoms they were accustomed to in exchange for security.

To accomplish this goal, Bush needed the right major crisis, or what the Project for the New American Century called, "a new Pearl Harbor."

Thanks to a group of CIA funded and trained operatives, Mr. Bush got his New Pearl Harbor ushering in a period of de facto martial law where the American Constitution was shredded and Americans were told resistance was futile. Before leaving office, the Bush Administration introduced another major crisis when the central banks of the world looted the national treasuries of their assets and left a legacy of <u>slavery to debt</u> for generations not yet born.

Bigger Government
Economically, America is on the brink of financial disaster as she has jettisoned her strength through independence and has bound herself to a faltering global economy. Our government leaders no longer adhere to a concept of obeying the spirit of the law, let alone the letter of the law. Most of them have no concept of right and wrong. No concept of what is and is not appropriate. And perhaps no conscience.

These politicians have no respect for the people who elected them. No respect for the American people. No respect for their office. No respect for the Constitution of the United States. No respect for what it means to be entrusted by the people of this nation to serve at the highest capacity. Their only goal is to consolidate more money and power into the hands of the few in order to control and manipulate the many.

Originally created to defend and protect, our government was now being asked to provide. As the problems grow, so must the government. Traditionally, Democrats have stood for big government, far-reaching federally controlled and federally funded programs and taxation at levels to match. One has to only scan through a few of Clinton's policies in <u>economic, spending, and tax</u>

strategy to see that sovereignty and freedom were the items actually targeted for reduction.

The governments ability to provide was demonstrated a few years later following the disaster left by hurricane Katrina. What emerged appeared to be more an operational test of "control" than of providing assistance.

We have witnessed over the past 100 years an ever increasing collectivist inspired transfer of wealth and a federal government takeover of the management of American business, health care, education and the American family. Clinton's actions demonstrated that he envisioned much more than mere renewal or reform; he wanted to create an entirely new society controlled by a massive collectivist government. George W. Bush flexed the collectivist muscle to bring the American population under the controlling wing of a government police state as he allowed the International banksters to siphon off Trillions of dollars of American assets.

America was ready for Change...

Barack Obama

The New World Order Messiah of Change
At that time many will turn away from the faith and will betray and hate each other, and many false prophets will appear and deceive many people. [Matthew 24:11]

Many of his supporters and most of the news media have presented Barack Obama as a miracle-working Messiah who promises to cure all ills for everyone.

Following his historic election as President of the United States it was not uncommon to witness his faithful followers in the throes of adoration fitting for a Messiah.

The day after Barack Obama was elected president, Larry Younginer knelt in front of the congregants at his suburban Atlanta church and offered a prayer of thanks. "Lord, we have again come to you in prayer, and you have heard our cries from heaven, and you have sent us again from the state called Illinois, a man called Barack to heal our land."

Barack Obama promised "CHANGE".

Setting the campaign rhetoric aside and looking instead at his cadre of advisors, I don't think the change Obama has in mind is what the American people had in mind when they blindly elected one of the most outspoken collectivists so far.

Within the first six weeks of office, Barack Obama proposed spending programs that exceeds the total government spending of the U.S. since it's founding to Obama's enaguguration. He has borrowed Trillions of dollars and ensured the slavery of our children for generations to come.

He sent his Secretary of State, Hillary Clinton, on a mission to China to beseech them to continue buying U.S. debt... and what did she use for collateral? Our children's lives and property.

One central tenant to the New World Order is the belief in creating a master race that rules the world.

For the New World Order, a world government is just the beginning. Once in place they can engage their plan to exterminate 80% of the world's population, while enabling the "elites" to live forever with the aid of advanced technology.

Shortly after being sworn in to office, this half white black faced president reversed Bush policies protecting innocent babies and opened the door for the mass extermination of millions of helpless lives around the world. Not only did he provide funding for Chinese style eugenics programs, he also lowered the barriers protecting unborn babies from being used as a commodity to be traded in the profitable scientific research market.

The Obama Deception

The Obama Deception is a hard-hitting film that completely destroys the myth that Barack Obama is working for the best interests of the American people. The Obama phenomenon is a hoax carefully crafted by the captains of the New World Order. He is being pushed as savior in an attempt to con the American people into accepting global slavery. We have reached a critical juncture in the New World Orders plans. Its not about Left or Right: its about a One World Government. The international banks plan to loot the people of the United States and turn them into slaves on a Global Plantation.

The Global Age is right upon us.

It is on the horizon of our lifetime.

This New World Order is not some prophetically speculative or futuristic fairy tale, but a real world reality. It is not some "wacko conspiracy theory" advanced by the fringe of society like the powers that be would have us believe. It is not a "conspiracy," rather it's an agenda. Anybody that will end their soma induced "holiday" and unplug from the delusional "matrix" will see the evidence all around them.

It has been a long time in the making, its pieces fitting into place from divergent realms and different players. Gears and levers of history have been moved and adjusted, and a large-scale game of Monopoly has been played, with real currency and real assets shifting hands - a game with very real winners and losers.

The players in this grand deception understand it is a dangerous and risky undertaking, for they are vastly outnumbered. If average Americans woke up and understood their true agenda, there would be an uprising of revolutionary proportions.

Therefore, demonizing the opposition and controlling people through disinformation and fear is critical as they conceal their true agenda. Published government documents characterize patriots as terrorists and a threat to law enforcement. World economic systems are threatened with catastrophic consequences unless the international banksters are allowed to consolidate their power into a global banking system.

"It is well the people of the nation do not understand our banking and monetary system, for if they did, I believe there would be a revolution before tomorrow morning." - Henry Ford

Even though the power of a small group of International bankers is colossal today according to Harvard and Princeton professor emeritus, Carroll Quigley, they are finding it increasingly difficult to conceal their true nature. He said of this group:

"Their aim is nothing less than to create a world system of financial control in private hands able to dominate the political system of each country and the economy of the world as a whole. The system was to be controlled in a feudalistic fashion by the central banks of the world acting in concert, by secret agreements arrived at in frequent private meetings and conferences." (Carroll Quigley, Tragedy and Hope (New York: The Macmillan Co., 1966)
Alas, a New World Order

While it is nearly impossible to accurately trace the interlocking agendas of these organizations, the supernatural dimension is the one that gives the puzzle meaning. While some may ascribe leadership of the New World Order to elitists's in the Bilderbergers, Trilateral Commission or Council of Foreign Relations, the truth is these people are mere pawns in a much grander agenda of the Antichrist.

He also forced everyone, small and great, rich and poor, free and slave, to receive a mark of his right hand or on his forehead, so that no one could buy or sell unless he had the mark, which is the name of the beast or the number of his name. [Revelation 13:16-17]

Scripture tells us of the establishment of a New World Order by the Antichrist in the last days. Indeed, the devil must have a dictatorial form of government if he is to rule the world. It is being slowly implemented in our governments through legislation and in our churches with a new spirituality until ultimately it will be in the hands of an elite of intelligent politically-connected religious-minded people in league with the Antichrist.

The Mark of the Beast

For a Real Time, Real Life example of the activities of The Beast, please have a look at "Cassiopaea Research Arm Under Attack," and read the articles linked from there, including "That Old Black MAJIC."

September 2001, a few days after the WTC disaster:
The headline of this morning's St. Petersburg Times says: $15-billion bailout set. The article proceeds to

inform us that "Congress passed a bailout plan Friday night to prevent the airline industry from collapsing." What's more, they did it with "extraordinary speed."

"Supporting our airlines is an act of patriotism," said Rep. Carolyn Maloney, D-N.Y."The Terrorists wanted to ground America, so we need to fly."
Aside from the fact that the only reason America has been grounded is because of an obvious effort to get us into a war, such specious reasoning simply astonishes me.

Well, the rhetoric gets even more preposterous: "We are not going to let our economy fail," said Rep. Clay Shaw, R-Fort Lauderdale.

I guess that this means that we are going to blame the economic plunge on the terrorist attack, right?
Nevertheless, this remark reminded me of something the C's once said about the "Mark of the Beast," and the reader may wish to have a look at the entire transcript on the "666" page. They remarked: "VI is 6 in Roman Numerals. S was 6 in ancient Egypt. A was 6 in Sanskrit. VISA, see, is 666. Interesting that to travel for extended periods one needs a "visa" also, yes?" And now, the issue of travel, (or lack thereof, is connected to the present activity of the U.S.A. Just what is in the works here?

Putting what the C's said together with my own ideas about the Who and What of the Beast, written back in 1986 and 87, I would like the reader to refer to that page as well, where I have used the book of Revelation to identify the "Home Base" of the Beast Empire. To boil it down, here are the pertinent excerpts:

The "Beast" has been, in accepted theological theory, long associated with, and identified as, the One Man Antichrist. This is due to a fundamental misunderstanding of the last verse of Revelation, Chapter 13.

One of the keys to unlocking the puzzle, as I mentioned, is the last verse of chapter 13. I had already figured out most of it but that last bit really had me stumped. I read the verse over and over and went back to the original Greek for clarification. I broke it down by syntax; rearranged it in numerous ways and went to bed exhausted by it one night. I awoke in the middle of the night with the word "Calculate" booming in my head and a vision of the word in large white letters against a black background. I jumped out of bed and grabbed my notes. "Calculate" was, indeed, the key.

Revelation 13, the chapter which describes the "Beast" begins:
"I stood on the sandy beach, I saw a beast coming up out of the sea with ten horns and seven heads. On his horns he had ten royal crowns and

blasphemous titles on his heads." This first sentence tells us of a landing on a foreign shore; the beast is to be found at a distance from the area of the previous chapter which describes the nation of Israel, the birth of Christ, and the persecutions of the church in Europe. To understand what John means by sea, we can look at chapter 16, verse 8: "The waters that you observed are races and multitudes..." (This is also interesting in light of the concept of people being wave-forms of the divine source). Examining all other references to beasts in the Bible, it is immediately apparent that, other than references to actual animals, this designation belongs to world empires.

Daniel's prophecies foreshadowed Revelation, and Daniel was told by an angel that a beast symbolized an empire. There is some interchangeability between "king" and "empire," just as there is interchangeability between "city" and "nation". This is also traditional since any king is considered diplomatically to be his country. I think that we can safely assume that John is not referring to a fantastic animal, so the only other supported interpretation we can give to this beast is that it is an empire.

John is most specific in describing the numbers of heads and horns and the placing of the crowns on the horns and not the heads! So, we must think this is to be of some import in describing the nature of this empire. Daniel, Chapter 7, describes his fourth beast as having ten horns and, it has been determined that Daniel's fourth beast was the Roman Empire. The beast in Chapter 12 of Revelation can also be identified, by its role, as the Roman Empire. The comparison can then be made that the crowns, in the case of the descriptions of the beast representing the Roman Empire, are upon the heads and not on the horns.

The number "7" is sacred among the Jews, indicating perfection or completion. It was used very often in a symbolic manner for the "whole" of a thing. Thus, seven heads would indicate an autonomous nation -- not under the rule of any other empire. The placement of the crowns on the horns rather than on the heads indicates that this is not a totalitarian, monarchial or dictatorial regime. The horns symbolize strength and the assembly of the people, for the horn was used to call the people to pray and to hear the words of the prophets. We can see that on this beast they represent the strength of an empire in the diversity of its people. Ten is symbolic of testing, an earthly foreshadowing of divine principle: "For since the law has merely a rude outline of the good things to come, instead of fully expressing those things, it can never perfect..."(Hebrews 10:1) So, we can conclude that the ten horns represents the assembling of a large number of people who express an almost divine concept in government -- since the rulership of the empire, symbolized by the crowns, is placed on the horns and not on the heads -- government of the people, by the people, for the people.

The heads, on the other hand, the decision making part of the beast, the administrative or titular head of an empire, are represented as having blasphemous titles on their foreheads. The definition of blasphemy is "profane usage of God's name". Profane simply means that which is not connected with religion. The blasphemous titles on the heads inform us that the government of this nation will use the name of God and purported spiritual principles to lead the people and present its policies.

"And the beast that I saw resembled a leopard, his feet were like those of a bear, and his mouth was like that of a lion."

Here we find that this new empire has many of the characteristics of former world empires as described by Daniel. The multiplicity of types also indicates the greater supremacy of this world empire. Possessing the military might of the Media-Persian empire as exemplified by the bear; the speed and cunning of Alexander's empire, the leopard; and the kingly nobility of the lion. That the mouth is described as being like a lion denotes loud and boastful speech as well -- self-aggrandizement and self-indulgence, and another meaning, as we shall see.

"And to him the dragon gave his might and power and his throne and great dominion."

The dragon is, classically, and in scripture, Satan. This sentence denotes the emerging character of this beast as well as establishes its position in the world. John says that the dragon gives his throne to the beast. This means that this empire becomes the number one nation on the earth in all things material: industry, commerce, political influence, economic living standards, arts, science, technology, material goods of all sorts and fleshly pleasures; all things pertaining to the "things of the world." That is not to say that any of these things are evil in themselves -- it is the attitude and ideal which is important as we will see further on.

John has informed us that the social structure of this end-time empire is controlled by a pervading principle of life that is antithetical to spirituality. The Dragon exalts this empire far above all the other societies of the world in all the things which pertain to materiality. This society is one which has set itself up as arbiter of what is right and wrong as well as being excessively preoccupied with physical appearance and material wealth and goods.

"And one of his heads seemed to have a deadly wound. But his death stroke was healed, and the whole earth went after the beast in amazement and admiration."

This verse tells us that one branch, or department of the administrative body suffers an attack. This attack is clarified in verse 14 which describes the wound as being inflicted by a sword -- a military action. Note that the verse says "seems" to have a deadly wound. This tells us that this event leads many to think that it is a death stroke and will finish the beast. Yet, the empire/beast recovers quickly and goes on to lead, and be adored by, an admiring world.

"They fell down and did homage to the dragon, because he had bestowed on the beast all his dominion and authority; they also praised and worshipped the beast, exclaiming, Who is a match for the beast, and who can make war against him?" To do homage means to serve or venerate, and this verse tells us that the benefits of Satan, materiality, as promulgated by the beast, become the standard of the other societies of the world. In addition, this verse identifies the ascendancy of materialism as occurring through military actions.

"And the beast was given the power of speech, uttering boastful and blasphemous words, and he was given freedom to exert his authority and to exercise his will during forty-two months." Recall in the previous chapter where Jesus is described as slaying nations with the breath of his mouth? We now have a clue as to the meaning of this remark.

Here we have the beast making war. "Speaking," in this context, clearly means war. And, having the mouth of a lion, we can be sure that this "speech" will be proud, haughty, and declaiming noble ideals. But, that this war/speech is blasphemous tells us that there is something hidden here that we must find, and we will a bit further on. The authority during 42 months is identified in verses three and four as military. Thus, claiming to act in the will or name of God, this nation will lead the peoples of the earth in a war for 42 months.

"He was further permitted to wage war on God's holy people and to overcome them. And power was given him to extend his authority over every tribe and people and tongue and nation."

This verse describes the extension of authority after the military action has ceased. Once again this nation is described as having the top position, and to a greater extent than before, in all material aspects. The results of the military action have served to place the beast in a position to "wage war against God's holy people." Contrary to popular theological opinion, I do not see these "Holy People" as members of any given denomination, "born again" or otherwise. God's people must be understood to be those who are members of His kingdom and, since this kingdom has not been externally established, being described as being within, we must look for another meaning to this usage.

Deuteronomy describes the nation of Israel as God's Holy People in its entirety. After the establishment of the "New Covenant", God's people are those who are "Circumcised in their hearts". Thus, the "Holy People" must be seen as those who manifest spiritual values over and above materialism. It might also be noted that Christ said, referring to little children, "of such is the kingdom of heaven"; so we may include the criteria of "becoming as a child" in order to be one of "God's Holy People." Children are born curious, adventurous, courageous and most especially, not hung up on "belief systems." Simple faith in the "rightness" of things, with no desire to "save" or change anything is one of the chief features of the "childlike" attitude.

The use of the word "overcome" in this context, informs us that an actual military action is not involved -- rather that the beast uses some means of inducement to cause innocent and unsuspecting individuals to fall into the ways of materialism. This is a war of forces - - materialism versus spirituality -- a severe attack on spiritual values, leading many astray. It also indicates that those who place spiritual values above material considerations will have a difficult time dealing with life in general due to the fact that only those who know how to "play the game" will be able to maneuver well in the society of the Beast.

"And all the inhabitants of the earth will fall down in adoration and pay him homage, every one whose name has not been recorded from the foundation of the world in the Book of Life of the Lamb that was slain from the foundation of the world."

This verse tells us that this empire will be victorious in propagating materialism over vast areas of the globe and that the ideals of independence from God, self-gratification and reliance on human wisdom and capabilities will come to be seen as the prevailing aspirations of the world. This does not mean that the entire world will attain these ideals, but that the economic, industrial, artistic, scientific achievements and living standards of this empire will be admired and emulated -- idolized, in fact.

However, we must also see that there will be some who do not fall into the trap set by the beast -- those who retain their ideals of spiritual perfection and achievement - - and that these people are foreordained to occupy this role.

"Whoever leads into captivity will himself go into captivity; if anyone slays with the sword, with the sword must he be slain. Herein is the patience and the faith and fidelity of the saints."

This caveat is inserted at this point for several reasons; The first is to reassure those who have been "foreordained" as well as those who have suffered actual death or loss, that what is sown is reaped. The beast is warned that nations invoke karma also!

"Then I saw another beast rising up out of the land; he had two horns like a lamb and he spoke like a dragon. He exerts all the power and right of control of the former beast in his presence, and causes the earth and those who dwell upon it to exalt and deify the first beast, whose deadly wound was healed, and worship him. He performs great signs -- startling miracles -- even making fire fall from the sky to the earth in men's sight. And because of the signs which he is allowed to perform in the presence of the first beast, he deceives those who inhabit the earth, commanding them to erect an image in the likeness of the beast which was wounded by the sword and still lived."

This second beast, must, once again, be an empire. However, it differs from the first beast in several ways which John describes in great detail. The first detail is the number of horns. Two is a number which has several meanings. First, it represents a minority, for two is the smallest number by which testimony may be accepted. Also, we may look to Genesis for some esoteric clarification:
"And God said, Let there be a firmament in the midst of the waters; and let it separate the waters below from the waters above .. and there was evening and morning, a second day." (Genesis 1:6,8, excerpts)

Here we see that the number two is related to a separating element which divides waters below from waters above. Throughout the Bible, water represents spirit and humanity.

In applying this principle to two horns, we see that the horns represent a powerful minority which acts in such a way as to separate mankind from his own spiritual heritage. This action comes about through things which appear harmless -- "appeared as a lamb" -- but are in actuality, propagating lies -- "speaks as a dragon"-- induces to material considerations. And, once again, speech refers to force, or violence so we may assume that this second beast has some relationship to making war or using force to dominate.

"He asserts all power and right of control of the former beast in his presence;"
...tells us that this powerful minority acts through and is supported by, the established empire of the first beast -- an empire within an empire. A minority which takes control by force and deception.

"Causes the earth and those who dwell upon it to exalt and deify the first beast, whose deadly wound was healed, and worship him"
...indicates that this second beast was behind the initiation of the military action described as a deadly wound and that this event was planned to bring the first beast into position to establish military supremacy and commercial world domination. This

establishment of military supremacy is emphasized in the lines:
"He performs great signs -- startling miracles -- even making fire fall from the sky to the earth in mens' sight"
...which describes the use of atomic weapons in this military action which lasts 42 months. This display of power is so awesome to the peoples of the world that they submit to the political and commercial domination of the first beast.

"And because of the signs which he is allowed to perform in the presence of the first beast, he deceives those who inhabit the earth, commanding them to erect an image in the likeness of the beast which was wounded by the sword and still lived."

The "image" of the beast has caused many a theologian to lose sleep. Understood in the context of this passage, we can perceive that this refers to the establishment of the principles of worldliness and materialism throughout the world. What is the image of the beast? Military might, speed and cunning, exalted position in worldly possessions and technology -- as described by John. That this ideal is extended around the earth through the lies, deception and force of the second beast, subverting other cultural ideals to materialism and using other nations politically, is what is being expressed by this verse -- and that it is the end result of the war in which the beast was wounded.

"And he was permitted to impart the breath of life into the beast's image so that the image of the beast could actually talk, and to cause to be put to death those who would not bow down and worship the image of the beast. Also, he compels all, both small and great, both rich and the poor, both free and slave, to be marked with an inscription on their right hands or on their foreheads, so that no one will have power to buy or sell unless he bears the stamp, the name of the beast or the number of his name."

The dreaded "Mark of the Beast." The horror of totalitarian world government -- tattoos, laser marks, implanted computer tapes -- a host of interpretations! Yet, we cannot look upon this lightly for it contains the implications of the most horrific prophetic curse ever delivered in the pages of scripture!

Before delving into the "Mark", let's look at the first portions of this section. The "breath of life" imparted to the image, or ideals of the beast, coupled with "speech" and "putting to death", express a repetition of the coupling of blasphemous speech and military action in the earlier verses. Thus we see that the beast will initiate "war" (active, cold, or covert) with those nations which do not adhere to its image, or domination in military and commercial respects. This is further amplified by the implications of buying and selling -- join the beast or die!

The first mention of a mark in the Bible occurs in Genesis 4:15: "And the Lord set a mark or sign upon Cain..."

It must be remembered that Cain was the first individual who asked: "Am I my brother's keeper?"

Job lamented,

"If I have sinned, what have I done you, O You watcher and keeper of men? Why have You set me as a mark for You so that I am a burden to myself?" (7:20)

Jeremiah cries:

"I am Jeremiah, the man who has seen affliction under the rod of His wrath. He has led me, and brought me into darkness, and not light. Surely He has turned away from me; His hand is against me all the day. My flesh and my skin has He worn out and made old; He has shattered my bones. He has built up against me, and surrounded me with bitterness, tribulation and anguish. He has caused me to dwell in dark places, as those long dead. He walled me about, so that I cannot get out; He has weighted down my chain. Also when I cry and shout for help, He shut out my prayer. He has enclosed my ways with hewn stone, He has made my paths crooked. He is to me like a bear lying in wait, and like a lion hiding in secret places. He has turned me off my ways, and pulled me in pieces; He has made me desolate. He has bent His bow, and set me as a mark for the arrow..." (Lamentations 3:1-12)

Ezekiel 9:4-6 says:

"And the Lord said to him, Go through the midst of the city, through the midst of Jerusalem, and set a mark upon the foreheads of the men who sigh and groan over all the abominations that are committed in the midst of it. And to the others He said in my hearing, Follow through the city, and smite: let not your eye spare, neither have any pity. Slay outright the elderly, the young man and the virgin, the infant and the women; but do not touch or go near any one on whom is the mark..."

And, Revelation says:
"Then another angel, a third, followed them, saying with a mighty voice, Whoever pays homage to the beast and his image and permits the stamp (mark) to be put on his forehead or on his hand, He too shall drink the wine of God's indignation and wrath, poured undiluted into the cup of His anger, and he shall be tormented with fire and brimstone in the presence of the holy angels and in the presence of the Lamb." (Revelation 14: 9-10)

"And the beast was seized and overpowered, and with him the false prophet who in his presence had worked wonders and performed miracles, (the second beast -- that which gives false testimony), by which he led astray those who had accepted or permitted to be placed upon them the stamp of the beast, and those who paid homage and gave divine honors to his image. Both of the two were hurled alive into the fiery lake that burns and blazes with brimstone." (Revelation 19:20)

"Then I saw a second angel ... saying, Harm neither the earth nor the sea nor the trees, until we have sealed the bond servants of our God upon their foreheads." (Revelation 7:2,3)

"Hear, O Israel: the Lord our God is one Lord -- the only Lord. And you shall love the Lord your God with all your heart, and with your entire being, and with all your might. And these words, which I am commanding you this day, shall be in your own mind and heart; you shall whet and sharpen them, so as to make them penetrate and shall talk of them when you sit in your house, and when you walk by the way, and when you lie down and when you rise up. And you shall bind them as a sign upon your hand, and they shall be as frontlets between your eyes, And you shall write them upon the doorposts of your house and on your gates." (Deuteronomy 6:4-9)

So, now we have a much clearer idea of what John means by the use of the word "mark" or "stamp," It is an ideological affiliation! A spiritual position! An attitude of mind, heart and action! Nothing more -- nothing less! What is it that one wears upon their forehead as a frontlet and binds upon their hand? The laws of God. What is one supposed to do with the laws of God? Whet and sharpen them -- use them and practice with them -- make them penetrate; interpret all of reality in these terms; teach them and make them the focal point of existence! This is the mark or seal of God.

And, the mark of the beast? The antithesis of the mark of God. The denial and rejection of the laws of God. The asking of the age-old question: Am I my brother's keeper?

We should note, however, that John divides the Mark of the beast into two categories: those who bear the "stamp" -- the name of the beast or those who bear the number of his name. And here we come to the final solution: the identity of the beast. For it is clear that the geographical area of this beast/empire is under sentence of doom as well as those who are marked by the esoteric significance of the number of the beast who are located elsewhere, geographically.

"Here is discernment -- a call for the wisdom; let anyone who has intelligence (penetration, insight) enough, CALCULATE the number of the beast; for it is a human number, the number of a certain man; his number is 666."
1. CALCULATE -- a mathematical operation. 2. Calculate what? -- The number of the beast.
3. Calculate how? -- a. it is a human number; b. the number of a certain man.
4. The unfinished numerical form of the name of the beast, the numbers which will give the mathematical result identical with the name number of the beast, thereby affirming identity, is 666.

The companion to the Torah, the Jewish collection of scripture, is the Kaballah. The Kaballah consists of many occult and esoteric teachings, one of which is a system of numerology. (It also includes astrological information.) In Kabbalistic tradition, a name number is very significant. Numbers were so important to the ancient Jews that an entire book is named "Numbers". They understood, as physicists do today, that numbers represent the closest we can ever come to writing and understanding the laws of the universe. In the past, a man's name number was so important that his name was often changed, signifying some important accomplishment or change of life, thereby changing the numerical value as well as the intrinsic meaning. A striking example is the change God made in the names of both Abraham and Sarah; formerly Abram and Sarai.

Clue 3a is clarified by 3b which indicates that we are not to interpret the former in literal terms -- the number of humanity being 6, according to Kaballah; but that we are to deal with a specific name just as if we were determining the name number of a certain, (any given) man. In presenting these clues, John is telling us that we are to use numerology to find the name number of the beast just as if it were a man. We may make this determination by matching our result with the result of the numerological application to the number 666. This will affirm our identification of the last great world empire --the Beast.

The symbology of these numbers is important in another way. The result of the rules of numerology applied to the number 666 is 9: 6+6+6=18; 1+8=9. Nine is not only the name number of the beast, it is the product of 3 squared, or divine completion. We can also see in these numbers man's attempt to usurp the position of God -- 6 repeated 3 times -- or the number of man arranged as the divine trinity. Symbolically nine signifies finality, completion, fulfillment. There are the nine beatitudes, nine gifts of the spirit, nine fruits of the spirit, and the words of Christ at the ninth hour: "It is finished!" This is echoed in Revelation: "Then the seventh angel emptied out his bowl into the air, and a mighty voice came out of the sanctuary of heaven from the throne, saying, It is done!" (16:17)

There are other clues to the meaning of the number nine. In the story of the ten lepers in Luke 17, only one, a Samaritan, turned back and thanked Jesus for his cleansing and Jesus asked "Were not ten cleansed? Where are the nine?" Was there no one found to return and to recognize and give thanks and praise to God except this alien?"

In Nehemiah 11, more light is shed upon the symbology of nine:
"Now the leaders of the people dwelt at Jerusalem; the rest of the people also cast lots, to bring one of ten to dwell in Jerusalem the holy city, while nine tenths dwelt in other towns and villages."

We may also observe that 9 is an inverted 6 and, expressing the idea of the law of God, in the triad, acting upon man who has "taken the seat in the temple" as describe previously (a triad of sixes) -- or 3 x 666 -- we get a most interesting product: 1998. This number is especially interesting in light of the prophecies of Nostradamus and Edgar Cayce. Using this date as a stepping off point, we might try adding or subtracting the 6.3 years of Daniel's prophesied tribulation. (The name "Daniel", by the way, is a nine -- a coincidence? I think not considering the many similarities of Revelation to Daniel!)

In 70 A.D. the Jewish temple was polluted and then destroyed. This was an archetype of what was to come. In the present time, the Temple is the body of mankind (naos vs. hieron) -- even the body of an individual. Our spiritual frequencies are being polluted by materialistic attitudes and this, as noted above, could be the key to the "Mark of the Beast."

Daniel wrote: "Then I heard a holy one speaking, and another holy one said to the one that spoke, For how long is the vision concerning the continual offering, the transgression that makes desolate, and the giving over of both the sanctuary and the host to be trampled under foot? And he said to him and to me, For two thousand and three hundred evenings and mornings; then the sanctuary shall be cleansed and restored."

Dividing 2300 by 365, we obtain the figure 6.3 years from that date, and, if that is the case, and the ending or beginning is 1998, then we try subtracting 6.3 years from 1998 and we find that the abomination that desolates will begin in late 1991. Or, on the other hand, the date could represent the beginning of destruction in which case we would add 6.3 years to 1998 finding that the end of tribulation would be in the year 2,004. [Laura's note added 3/23/2000:

1998 was the most violent year in the history of weather and ended as the hottest year ever recorded. Also, a minor recession occurred in 1998 concurrent with the Persian Gulf conflict, which might have been "markers" for those with eyes to see. Could THIS be the beginning of the "abomination of desolation?"]

What does Jesus say about the abomination that desolates?

"So when you see the appalling sacrilege spoken of by the prophet Daniel standing in the Holy Place, let the reader take notice and ponder and heed this, Then let those who are in Judea flee to the mountains; Let him who is on the housetop not come down and go into the house to take anything; and let him who is in the field not turn back to get his overcoat. And also for the women (souls) who are pregnant (spiritually unformed) and for those who have nursing babies in those days! (Those who are not yet ready for the meat of truth) For then there will be great tribulation -- affliction, distress and oppression -- such as has not been from the beginning of the world until now; no, and never will be again. If those days had not been shortened, no human being would endure and survive; but for the sake of the elect (God's chosen ones) those days will be shortened.

"For just as the lightening flashes from the east and shines and is seen as far as the west, so will the coming of the Son of Man be... Immediately after the tribulation of those days the sun will be darkened, and the moon will not shed her light, and the stars will fall from the sky, and the powers of the heavens will be shaken. Then the sign of the Son of Man will appear in the sky, and then all the tribes of the earth will mourn and beat their breasts and lament in anguish, and they will see the Son of Man coming on the clouds of heaven with power and great glory -- in brilliancy and splendor." (Matthew 24:15-30)
[Laura's note added 03/23/2000: So, the year 2004 doesn't look good!]

The prophecies of Revelation state that the beast will be cast into the lake of fire along with the false prophet. This becomes meaningful when we remember Velikovsky's "rains and rivers of fire," or flaming naptha which would be concomitant with an encounter with a comet of a certain type. Thus, the geographical area of the Beast Empire, and those who are doomed throughout the globe for their lack of spiritual "clothing," may have some problems, to say the least. And, considering the figure of Noah as well as the parable of the ten lepers along with the archtypal example from Nehemiah, we must understand that few may survive! One tenth, perhaps, of the earth's population of over five billion!

Now, you ask, Who -- or What -- is the Beast? Which world empire fits the descriptions of Revelation 13?

Which world empire began on a foreign shore, formed of many races and tongues; (primarily people from the area of the old Roman Empire -- the "Little Horn" of Daniel, which made war with three of the ten divisions of the Roman Empire: England, France and Spain)?

Which nation on the earth rapidly became the richest and most powerful empire on earth, using the name of God as its motto?

Which nation suffered a military attack which seemed to be devastating, but was, in fact, a political manipulation designed to engender popular support for a war of greed -- a wound which healed so quickly that one can't help but wonder if all preparations were made in advance?

Which nation rose up after such an attack and went on to lead an adoring world in a global war, winning on two fronts simultaneously? A war which involved this empire for a period of 42 months?

Which empire developed and used "fire falling from the sky in the sight of men" -- atomic weapons -- to awe and intimidate the peoples of the world?

Which nation used such a blasphemous power on a people already defeated, after having deliberately drawn them into war?

Which nation, after this war, established, and still maintains, military presence and industrial outposts over all the globe and has made the world its marketplace -- a financial bonanza -- propagating materialism as though it were manna from heaven or the word of God in order to satiate its voracious appetite for money and power?

What nation on the earth is ruled from behind the political stage by the industrial-military complex -- a group so powerful they can politically (or literally) assassinate public and private figures with impunity; a group of wealthy elitists who know no bounds to their greed; a group which foments social unrest, political strife, unstable economies, wars and revolutions; a group which stimulates technology and promulgates materialism, to keep their pockets full and the strings of power in their hands?

What nation on earth has been manipulated by the electronic media -- under the control of the motivation masters hired by the industrial-military complex (the false prophets of materialism and technology) -- so that they have lost sight of the spirit and meaning of those ideals which gave birth to their empire?

What nation's name number is NINE?

Did you figure it out? Use the following table to give values to the letters, then add them all together, continuing to add until you are left with a single digit. After you have tried all sorts of names and combinations, try United States (of) America. (Omit the "of" as it is not part of the name proper.)

1 2 3 4 5 6 7 8 9
A B C D E F G H I
J K L M N O P Q R
S T U V W X Y Z

Initially, when I discovered this funny relationship, I immediately discarded it for the simple reason that the Book of Revelation was written in Greek and I was calculating in English. But, after giving it some thought, I realized that if I was going to give even a modicum of credibility to a 2000 year old prophecy, that I ought to also give some consideration that such a prophecy COULD, indeed, accommodate the language factor. After all, if I am thinking that events so far in the future can be foreseen, certainly the prophetic ideation would naturally include the fact that the lingua Franca of the future time was English.

Years ago it occurred to me that it was most peculiar that the United States was not taught as being included or mentioned in the great Biblical prophecies. Since it was apparent to me that it has become the most powerful and influential nation on the face of the planet, I thought this rather strange. This was due, as it was explained to me, to the fact that the prophecies concerned, mainly, the Jews and, having been delivered through Jews, primarily concerned those events which affected the Israeli people. Yet, we are talking about prophecies which are global in import. Again I say, if we are going to take, as a working hypothesis, the idea that prophetic abilities exist at all and that they can operate thousands of years into the future, then we must also accept that those same prophetic abilities will be able to perceive the major actors in the cosmic drama of the future. And, if the drama is played out on the stage of the entire globe, then we must understand that the discussion will, of necessity, involve the stars of the play.

John, having brought the United States into his prophecy in Revelation 13, continues with his theme, describing the destructions of war and cosmic upheaval in chapters 14, 15, and 16. He then moves in for a close-up of an interaction which is very important for it further amplifies the roles of various participants in the end-time events.

Chapters 17 and 18 deal with the identification and descriptions of destruction of an entity known as the "Great Harlot".

Many have interpreted this woman to represent the Catholic Church, all denominational churches, occultists, and so forth. However, careful analysis of this and related portions of scripture will show that this is neither appropriate nor in keeping with the global sense of the prophecy. (And, in a previous chapter, we described the apostate condition of the Christian Churches.)

Scripturally, "Woman" means either the spiritual half of the human totality -- the union of male and female -- or, in an expanded view, "woman" symbolizes the socio-cultural-political manifestations of a group, a city, a nation.

Isaiah addresses the nation of Israel in a foreshadowing of John's prophecy:
"How the faithful city has become an idolatrous harlot, she who was full of justice ... Your princes are rebels and companions of thieves; every one loves bribes and runs after compensation and rewards. They judge not for the fatherless nor defend them, neither does the cause of the widow come to them." (1:21,23)
Ezekial uses the same terms and expands the theme:
"...You ate fine flour and honey and oil ... Your reknown went forth among the nations for your

beauty ... But you trusted and relied on your own beauty ... You have made your beauty an abomination ... You have played the harlot also with the Assyrians, because you were insatiable ... You multiplied your harlotry with the land of trade, with Chaldea; and yet even with this you were not satisfied ... Because of all the idols of your abominations, and for the blood of your children that you gave to them ... I will gather all your lovers ... They shall throw down your vaulted place, and shall demolish your high places ... They shall stone you and thrust you through with swords ... They shall burn your houses ... As is the mother, so is her daughter ... Your mother was a Hittite and your father an Amorite ... Your elder sister is Samaria ... your younger sister is Sodom ... You were more corrupt in all your ways than they were ... The iniquity of Sodom: pride, overabundance of food, prosperous ease and idleness were hers and her daughters; neither did she strengthen the hand of the poor and needy.." (Chapter 16, excerpts)

Here we have a wealth of background for interpreting the "Harlot" in John's prophecy. We may observe that "harlotry" relates, in a well defined sense, to materialism. I also, at this point, want to call attention to an obscure reference in Revelation 11:18 which says:
"The great city which is in a spiritual sense called by the names of Sodom and Egypt, where also their Lord was crucified."

It is obvious that Christ was not crucified in either Sodom or Egypt, but Jerusalem; and John makes it plain that this "city" is re-enacting, in a spiritual sense, the sins of all three. Noting the "sins" of Sodom and Egypt in the foregoing passages as well as the concept that the United States is taking the global role of Israel, and, understanding that the terms "city" and "nation" are very often interchangeable, we may arrive at a conclusion as to which nation this multiple reference applies. Revelation 17 begins:

"One of the seven angels who had the seven bowls came and spoke to me saying, Come with me! I will show you the doom of the Great Harlot who is seated on many waters, with whom the rulers of the earth have joined in prostitution, and with the wine of whose immorality the inhabitants of the earth have become intoxicated."

This passage gives us the clues that this "harlotry", or materialism, is worldwide and that the leaders of the earth are guilty of the specific sins of greed, perversion of justice, oppression of the poor and helpless, unfair trade practices, graft and governmental corruption as defined by Ezekial. Sound familiar?

So, we see a socio-cultural-political condition of harlotry which promulgates the idea of human technological achievement as the ultimate aspiration for mankind. This woman, or spiritual state of mankind, is further described as "seated on a scarlet beast covered with blasphemous titles, with seven heads and ten horns. The woman was robed in purple and scarlet, and bedecked with gold, precious stones and pearls, holding in her hand a cup of gold full of the accursed offenses and the filth of her lewdness and vice." The nation which is the seat, or foundation, of this corrupt spiritual ideal, described as a beast with seven heads and ten horns, harkens back to the beast of chapter 13. The colors are significant in that they represent government and religion -- scarlet being the priestly color and purple being the governing color -- and tell us that both the beast and, to a greater extent, the woman are revered by the peoples of the earth. Anyone who doubts that materialism has become a god in our society should try a little experiment: Try, for a period of twenty minutes each day, to clear the mind entirely and simply experience the quietness of the spirit. Nine people out of ten will have great difficulty quieting their thoughts and kicking them out, so to speak. Those thoughts which return to you most frequently, those ideas which are most persistent in holding your mind are, in truth, your god.

Some people think about sports, some people cannot stop thinking about their future plans in regards to making money, acquiring possessions, furthering relationships and rehashing past events. But, it will be seen, in the final analysis, that the main obstacle to meditation, or quieting the mind and contemplating spirit, is money -- either the getting, keeping, or spending of it. Whatever the consciousness drifts to naturally is the individual's ideal.

The gold, the jewels and the pearls adorning the Harlot tell us that all the mental and spiritual achievements of the earth are centered upon materialism -- this includes science, education, arts, culture, music and all other aspects of human potential -- including religion.

"And on her forehead was inscribed a name of mystery -- with a secret symbolic meaning: Babylon the great, the mother of prostitutes and of the filth and atrocities and abominations of the earth." Babylon was the great city which arose in Chaldea, "the land of trade." This verse tells us that this harlotry -- materialism -- gives rise to unspeakable crimes which individuals undertake to further their pursuit of sensual pleasure and acquisition of material goods. The deepest and most abominable sense of this description relates to warfare.

Many books have been written which expose the fact that governments do not wage war for moral or even ideological reasons -- wars are simply acts of greedy materialism -- but this is not commonly known among the masses for most of them do not read. Many still believe that the American Revolution, the Civil War, World Wars I and II were fought to defend noble ideals, and such people have been so thoroughly indoctrinated and duped on this subject that the mere mention of the actual facts causes them to close their ears and minds and live their lives in blissful ignorance, contaminating their children with unfounded patriotic zeal, and producing more fodder for the cannons.

One of the most abhorrent practices engaged in by ancient peoples, including, on occasion, the Israelites, was human sacrifice -- in particular child sacrifice. It seems that we, in the present age, continue to pass our innocent offspring "through the fire" with as little regard as did the ancients -- only now we call it "noble patriotism."

I would like to suggest that governments and their industrial military masters are fornicators and the "Great Harlot", the great, dark and evil system of materialism, is their mistress. Materialism is the mother of war, famine, disease, ignorance, drug addiction, murder, robbery, rape, and a host of assorted other evils of our day. Thus they are indeed drunk on the blood of martyrs.

"I also saw that the woman was drunk, with the blood of the saints, and the blood of the martyrs for Jesus. And when I saw her I was utterly amazed and wondered greatly. But the angel said to me, Why do you wonder? I will explain to you the mystery of the woman, as well as the beast having the seven heads and ten horns that carries her. The beast that you saw was, but is no more, and he is going to come up out of the abyss and proceed to go to perdition; this calls for a mind with wisdom and intelligence -- it is something for a particular mode of thinking and judging of thoughts, feelings and purposes. The seven heads are seven hills upon which the woman is sitting; and they are also seven kings, five of whom have fallen, one still exists, the other has not yet appeared, and when he does arrive he must stay a brief time. And as for the beast that was but now is no more, he is an eighth ruler, but he is of the seven and belongs to them, and he goes to perdition." A caveat is inserted into this explanation which tells us that the answer is hidden and is in the form, once again, of a riddle. It is like the old conundrum:

"Down in the dark dungeon, I saw a bright light; all saddled, all bridled, all set for a fight. Now I've told you the answer three times in a row: what did I see?" And the answer?

"All."

The first, and obvious, interpretation is that "seven hills" relates to Rome -- the "City of Seven Hills" -- and this is where most interpreters lose their way. Seven is also seven kings, or empires, five of which had fallen at the time John wrote Revelation. These can be identified as: Egypt, Assyria, Babylon, Media-Persia, and Greece. The sixth, Rome, was in power at the time of John's vision. The seventh "has not yet appeared, and when he does arrive, he must stay but a brief time." And, the eighth is "of the seven and belongs to them."

There is a very important transition indicated here in the number symbologies. Recall that the number seven is the number of perfection -- the whole of a thing. We know that the sixth "king" or empire, is Rome; but who is the seventh, which completes the number, and how does the eighth fit in. This is why John said this was going to be tricky!

The "seventh" empire is the Holy Roman Empire, which, as a truly great empire only lasted for a brief time. The Holy Roman Empire was part of the original Roman Empire, and its subsequent conquerors and rulers were scions of Rome in fact as well as philosophy. The eighth is the present United Sates government which "belongs" to the seven in that it was a British Crown Colony, and our form of government, language and social customs derive from England which took them from Rome. Britain also rejected the overlordship of the Church of Rome, the power behind the Holy Roman Empire, rather earlier than the Continental European countries, so can be seen as the root and even a "part" of the "eighth" empire. It could also be, in stricter terms, the seventh in and of itself. The United States also belongs to the former "Seven" in that it embodies all the power and corruption of all the former empires put together and is the natural heir of them all.

The beast which "was, but is no more, and is going to come up out of the abyss" is identified by seven hills, (Rome), and is also the eighth -- of the seven and belonging to them; eight being the number of regeneration -- which identifies it as a "reincarnation" of the Roman Empire, but also connects it to Belshazzar in the Book of Daniel. If you recall, the king saw the handwriting on the wall and called for wise men and interpreters. Daniel interpreted the writing:

"O king, the Most High God gave Nebuchadnezzar your father a kingdom and greatness and glory and majesty; And because of the greatness that He gave him, all peoples, nations, and languages trembled and feared before him... But when his heart was lifted up, and his mind and spirit were hardened so that he dealt proudly, he was deposed from his kingly throne, and his glory was taken from him; He was driven from among men, and his heart and mind was made like the beasts..." (Daniel 5:18,21, exc.) This is the "beast" John meant when he spoke of the one which was cast into the abyss. Nebuchadnezzar and the empire he represented. This indicates that this beast which is to come will also have major aspects of the Babylonian influence, which is to glorify materialism.

However, John indicates that this is not as simple as it would appear. John is prophesying global events using archetypes familiar to him and, we have already conjectured that the United States is a cumulative re-enactment of Israel, Sodom, Egypt and now, Rome and Babylon. This relates, in a sense, to the multiple animal identities of the beast of Chapter 13. Just as that beast was composed of many aspects of various animals, so, now, we find the same concept expressed in terms of socio-cultural manifestations.

Every aspect of the United States is in agreement with these varied descriptions -- from our government style (Roman), to our trade practices (Babylon), to our sensuality (Egyptian), to our pride, over-abundance, and prosperous ease and idleness (Sodom).

Additionally, we may observe that a nation which spends billions of dollars annually to fund warfare and space exploration while millions of its own citizens go without adequate food, clothing, housing and medical care, has, somehow, lost sight of the priorities which make an empire truly great.

John continues:

"Also, the ten horns that you observed are ten rulers who have as yet received no royal dominion, but together they are to receive power and authority as rulers for single hour along with the beast. These have one common policy and they deliver their power and authority to the beast. They will wage war with the Lamb, and the Lamb will triumph over them; for He is Lord of lords and King of kings, and those with Him and on His side are chosen and called and loyal and faithful followers." As noted in the previous chapter, ten is the number which represents an earthly foreshadowing of divine principle and, as such, exemplifies human law. In this passage, John amplifies the meaning of the ten horns -- the ten rulers, or dominions, with no authority which receive power along with the beast -- as representing the ten major divisions of the Roman Empire from which America drew its populace. John states that they ruled with the beast and then delivered their power to the beast, having one common policy -- or, stated in more modern terms, created a democracy.

This verse reveals that, initially, the peoples, or horns, which constitute the nation of the beast, had authority and power, but, at some point early on, delivered their authority over to the beast -- established a federal government. The term "common policy", prior to this event, describes a former state of true democracy -- relinquished to the beast. This point may be hotly disputed by those who have been stupefied by the media and believe that we have lived and continue to live, in a democracy set up by the Constitutional Convention of 1787.

M.L. Wilson wrote in Democracy Has Roots, that the Constitution was "a remarkable achievement in the avoidance of majority rule."

It is not surprising that the ratification of this Constitution was popularly opposed. The conventioneers promised to amend it at the first regular session of Congress. These promised amendments came to be known as the "Bill of Rights" and it is in these first ten amendments that Americans have their supposed "Constitutional Rights." A sobering thought when one considers that amendments have been repealed in the past. But for the "Bill of Rights," hundreds of years of blood-letting for personal liberty would have been tossed on the trash heap by the Federal Government, the Beast to whom the ten horns, the Assembly of People, gave their authority.

This beast, blasphemously using God's name to further its policies and plans, rapidly propagated the ideals of materialism and capitalism. And, in a process of unadulterated propaganda, these ideals have been inextricably linked with "democracy" as though the two were identical.

The result of this has been a vast chasm between the "haves" and the "have-nots" which grows wider and deeper every day, while the former continue to dupe the latter into believing and sacrificing for that which does not exist.

"And the angel further said to me, the waters that you observed where the harlot is seated, are races and multitudes and nations and dialects. And the ten horns that you saw, they and the beast will hate the harlot; they will make her cheerless and they will strip her, and eat up her flesh and utterly consume her with fire. For God has put it into their hearts to carry out His own purpose by acting in harmony in surrendering their royal power and authority to the beast, until the prophetic words -- intentions and promises -- of God shall be fulfilled. And the woman that you saw is herself the great city which dominates and controls the rulers and the leaders of the earth." In order to get the correct sense of this portion of Revelation, we must organize the words in a more "English" syntactical order:

"For God has put it into their hearts to carry out His own purpose by acting in harmony in surrendering their royal power and authority to the beast, until the prophetic words, -- intentions and promises -- of God shall be fulfilled. And the woman that you saw is herself the great city which dominates and controls the rulers and leaders of the earth. The waters that you observed, where the harlot is seated, are races and multitudes and nations and dialects. And the ten horns that you saw, they and the beast will hate the harlot; they will make her cheerless and they will strip her, and eat up her flesh and utterly consume her with fire." It is fairly simple to see the relationship between John's Great City: "Babylon" and Nostradamus' "Great New City" and relate both appellations to New York, though in the greater sense it means the entire nation just as Jerusalem means the entire nation of Israel.

At about the same time that the American Revolution was being fought, a man name Adam Weishaupt founded an organization in Europe dedicated to the idea that only the elite were fit to rule and it was the duty of these elite to band together and manipulate international affairs to this end. This organization was formed according to the format laid down by the Society of Jesus -- circles within circles - and its code was expressed in Masonic terms. They were found out, raided and, supposedly disbanded. However, there is evidence that they simply went underground. It might be conjectured that the framers of our constitution were aware of and even participated in such ideological "clubs".

In the early part of the 20th century, certain members of this organization, affiliated with eminent European International Banking families, emigrated to this country. Evidence exists that these individuals promoted the ideas and ideals of Weishaupt's "Order of Illuminati" among the wealthy elite of America. Prior to this time, there were disorganized attempts to control the machinations of government by the wealthy elite. This was deplored by Andrew Jackson, our seventh president, who wrote:

"I am one of those who do not believe that a national debt is a national blessing, but rather a curse to a republic; inasmuch as it is calculated to raise around the administration a moneyed aristocracy dangerous to the liberties of the country." This brings us to the crux of the matter: Money.

One of the downfalls of democracy in the early history of this country was money. Governments have always spent far more money than they could get from taxation. In order to finance their projects, (including war, graft and corruption), they must issue bonds. A small percentage of these bonds are held by ordinary private citizens; the majority are held by International Bankers. This is called the National Debt.

When any given individual borrows money from a bank, they usually provide collateral. When a large business or corporation borrows money, they too, provide collateral -- which usually consists in placing members of the lending institution on their board and permitting the lender to direct, or control, some of the corporate policies.

In this way, governments are like corporations -- their policies are controlled by the money-lenders. The money-lenders have another means of assuring that the government keeps in line with its policies -- by funding the enemy. In this way, political power is balanced and all power lies in the hands of the lender. Since it is evidently politic for enemies to be kept in a tense state to assure the bankers of their profits, it can be seen that political and social tensions are fomented for financial gain. This is exactly the case, and this is the game that has been played between governments for hundreds of years with the bankers in the background pulling the strings.

On many occasions, this game has resulted in vast, money-making operations called wars, which have taken literally millions of lives.

The group which formed among the wealthy elite in this country as a result of the propagandizing of the European Illuminati soon began manipulating the economy of the U.S. and a "panic" ensued on Wall Street which set the country up to accept "banking reforms". Since the wealthy elite were not popular among the masses, they realized that they must not openly advocate such reforms and, in fact, erected a smoke-screen of protest -- feeling this to be the surest way of obtaining popular support. The ruse worked and the Federal Reserve System was enacted.

Henry Cabot Lodge, Sr., said: "The bill as it stands seems to me to open the way to a vast inflation of currency... I do not like to think that any law can be passed which will make it possible to submerge the gold standard in a flood in irredeemable paper currency." But, it was passed.

Our "Central Bank" controls our money supply and interest rates. It can create inflation or deflation at will -- recession or boom. And, the title of this system is misleading -- no part of the federal government controls the Federal Reserve! This was admitted by Secretary of the Treasury, David M. Kennedy, in an interview, May 5, 1969. The Federal Reserve has never been audited, either. How successful is the Federal Reserve system? When Woodrow Wilson took office, the national debt was $1 billion. Even considering our increase in population, a national debt in the trillions staggers acceptance. But, from the point of view of the bankers, this is progress as they now own the county!

What is the ultimate goal of this group of wealthy elitists?

"A conspiratorial network is revealed in Tragedy and Hope, by Professor Carroll Quigley, Foreign Service School, Georgetown University, formerly of Princeton and Harvard: 'I know of the operations of this network because I have studied it for twenty years and was permitted for two years, in the early 1960's to examine its papers and secret records. I have no aversion to it or to most of its aims and have, for much of my life, been close to it and to many of its instruments. I have objected, both in the past and recently, to a few of its policies... but in general my chief difference of opinion is that it wishes to remain unknown, and I believe its role in history is significant enough to be known.'" The professor goes on to describe the aims of the network as being nothing short of control of the entire world through the respective governments of individual countries by means of economics.

"In other words, this power mad clique wants to rule the world. Even more frightening, they want total control over all individual actions. As professor Quigley observes: '...His (the individual's) freedom and choice will be controlled within very narrow alternatives by the fact that he will be numbered from birth and followed, as a number, through his educational training, his required military or other public service, his tax contributions, his health and medical requirements, and his final retirement and death benefits.' This group wants control over all natural resources, business, banking and transportation by controlling the governments of the world. In order to accomplish these aims the conspirators have had no qualms about fomenting wars, economic depressions and international hatred. They want a monopoly which would eliminate all competitors and destroy the free enterprise system. And Professor Quigley of Harvard, Princeton and Georgetown approves! [Gary Allen, None Dare Call it Conspiracy] And, since 1945, where has this group of wealthy elitists centered their operation? New York -- the marketplace and cultural center of the world! And, how far do their operations extend? Around the globe! And, who are the members? Over 1500 members around the globe representing the lions of industry, communication, politics, economics etc.

It may be apparent by this time that the "Harlot" is a creation of the "Second Beast" of Revelation 13, and, because of the deceptive, controlling tactics of this entity, we may also understand the sense in which John addresses it as the "false Prophet."

However, up to the present, the propaganda of the "False Prophet" has been for "Materialistic Capitalism."

There is a definite and sudden change noted in both Revelation 13 and Revelation 17.

In Revelation 13, John speaks of the "worship" or "reverence" given to the "image" of the beast. This act is connected with numbers and, in addition to the already discussed esoteric interpretation of these numbers, we must examine another facet.
The probability is that our government, as well as other governments of the earth will, in unity, move to a "cashless" society, and that all financial transactions will be handled by computer based upon a number assigned to the individual at birth. In the U.S. we have, at the present time, the social security number which is a series of nine digits. Quite recently, legislation was passed which made the obtaining of this number mandatory for income tax purposes. And, income tax is legally mandated. (It must be noted that a graduated income tax and a "Central Bank" are two of the ten planks of the Communist Manifesto, but I don't think we are here talking about the instituting of communism; rather a total Oligarchy.)

If we view the instituting of the "Mark of the Beast" as the onset of hidden totalitarianism, we must then see the destruction of the "Harlot" as popular opposition and revolution against same.

The materialism of the "Harlot", as defined in Ezekiel, is that which oppresses the masses for the enrichment of the few. And, since the ten horns and the Beast, or the empire, "eat up the flesh" of the harlot, at the time of the end, we may see this to be some sort of major disruption in the order of things, though whether it is military or revolutionary actions within our own country, or extra-terrestrial events activated by the "contact potential difference" imbalance of the planetary sphere is hard to tell. Additionally, the harlot is seated on "many waters" so we may infer that this indicates global events.

That this is to be a global event, is amplified in Chapters 14 an 18. Chapters 14, 15 and 16 are a broad overview of the final conflicts leading up to the ultimate cosmic cataclysm. Chapter 18 is a close-up of the fate of the Harlot.

"Then another angel, a second, followed, declaring, Fallen, fallen is Babylon the great! She who made all nations drink of the wine of her passionate unchasitity. Then another angel, a third, followed them, saying with a mighty voice, Whoever pays homage to the beast and his image and permits the stamp to be put on his forehead or on his hand, He too shall drink of the wine of God's indignation and wrath... Again I looked, and lo, a white cloud, and sitting on the cloud One resembling a Son of man, with a crown of gold on His head, and a sharp scythe in His hand... So he Who was sitting upon the cloud swung His scythe on the earth and the earth's crop was harvested. And another angel came forth from the altar, who has authority and power over fire, and he called with a loud cry to him who had the sharp scythe. Put forth your scythe and reap the fruitage of the vine of the earth, for its grapes are entirely ripe. So the angel swung his scythe on the earth and stripped the grapes and gathered the vintage from the vines of the earth, and cast it into the huge wine press of God's indignation and wrath. And the wine presses were trodden outside the city, and the blood poured from the wine press, as high as horses bridles, for a distance of one thousand and six hundred stadia (about two hundred miles)." (Rev. 14, exc.) There are several images here which lend credence to the idea of global cataclysm. The first is the "white clouds" and the second is the image of the angel with the scythe. But, the possibility or war or revolution exists as well, considering the "cloud like" appearance of atomic explosions and the distance of destruction around the city, 200 miles, is entirely in keeping with models of nuclear destruction.

"She is fallen. Mighty Babylon is fallen... Because all nations have drunk the wine of her passionate unchastity, and the rulers and leaders of the earth have joined with her in committing fornication, and the businessmen of the earth have become rich with the wealth of her excessive luxury and wantonness. Repay to her what she herself has paid and double in accordance with what she has

done." (Rev. 18, exc.) This reminds us of Revelation 13:
"Whoever leads into captivity will himself go into captivity; if any one slays with the sword by the sword must he be slain." And, considering the United States' use of nuclear weaponry upon the already defeated Japanese people, this does not bode well for our nation. Also, we must consider the evils of the propagating of materialism which has seduced the nations into forgetting their priorities -- spiritual development being the primary one. The scriptures say God is not mocked; whatsoever a man sows, that will he also reap -- and we may assume this to apply to nations, as well.

"To the degree that she glorified herself and reveled in her wantonness -- living deliciously and luxuriously -- to that measure impose on her torment and anguish and tears and mourning. Since in her heart she boasts, I am not a widow; as a queen I sit, and I shall never see suffering or experience sorrow." (Rev. 18, ex.)

The fate of the Harlot, the Beast, the False Prophet, all aspects of the same national entity, are cataclysmic as described by John.

"So shall her plagues come thick upon her in a single day, pestilence, and anguish and sorrow and famine, and she shall be utterly consumed -- burned up with fire; for mighty is the Lord God Who judges her. And the rulers and leaders of the earth, who joined her in her immorality and luxuriated with her, will weep and beat their breasts and lament over her when they see the smoke of her conflagration. They will stand a long way off, in terror of her torment, and they will cry, Woe and Alas! The Great City, Babylon! In one single hour how your doom has overtaken you! And the earth's businessmen weep and grieve over her because no one buys their freight any more... In one hour (Babylon) has been destroyed and become a desert!"

Is this all John sees? The end of Babylon? We may recall at this time that Nostradamus predicted the coming of "The Great King of Terror" in the sky which then enabled the arising of the "King of the Mongols". Revelation describes a similar event in great detail, and it is described as occurring after the destruction of Babylon.

"Then I saw another wonder in heaven, great and marvelous. There were seven angels bringing seven plagues, which are the last, for with them God's wrath is completely expressed -- reaches its climax and is ended... I saw what seemed to be a glassy sea blended with fire... (Recall the rivers and rains of flaming petroleum)... and the sanctuary of... heaven was thrown open and there came out of the temple sanctuary the seven angels bringing the seven plagues; They were arrayed in pure gleaming linen, and around their breasts they wore girdles of gold... And the sanctuary was filled with smoke from the glory of God and from His might and power... So the first angel went and emptied his bowl on the earth, and foul and painful ulcers came on the people who were marked with the stamp of the beast and who did homage to his name." (Rev. 15, 16, exc.)

In fact that these plagues seem to be specific to a certain group, namely those "marked" by the beast, is a curious statement. Could this indicate that this is due to the adherence of ideology? An individual who is so materialistic that he will not admit to the possibility of spiritual and prophetic truth, will do nothing to prepare for cataclysm and will, therefore, be unprepared to deal with it and will suffer the range of events unmitigated. Additionally, this idea seems to indicate that most of the destructive events will occur on the Western portion of the globe.

"The second angel emptied his bowl into the sea, and it turned into blood like that of a corpse, ill-smelling and disgusting, and everything that was in the sea perished. Then the third angel emptied out his bowl into the rivers and the springs of water, and they turned into blood. Then the fourth angel emptied out his bowl upon the sun, and it was permitted to burn humanity with heat... Then the fifth angel emptied his bowl on the throne of the beast, and his kingdom was plunged in darkness, and people gnawed their tongues for the torment... Then the sixth angel emptied his bowl on the mighty river Euphrates, and its water was dried up to make ready a road for the kings of the east..." (Rev. 16, ex.)

All of these effects describe the actions of a comet upon the earth as described in Velikovsky's Worlds in Collision. The "drying of the Euphrates" probably indicates an alteration of the geography of the earth which will enable the peoples of the Orient to emerge as dominant which, by the implications of this statement taken with the foregoing passage relating to the destruction of Babylon, might be involved in some conflict at the time the comet heads their way, disrupting their conflict at least temporarily.

"And I saw three loathsome spirits like frogs, from the mouth of the dragon and from the mouth of the beast and from the mouth of the false prophet. For really they are the spirits of demons that perform signs. And they go forth to the rulers and leaders all over the world, to gather them together for war on the great day of God the Almighty... And they gathered them together at the place which in Hebrew is called Armageddon." (Rev. 16, ex.)

Now why, one must ask, in the name of all good sense, would the nations of the earth gather together for the long prognosticated war called "Armageddon," in the midst of cosmic upheaval? Maybe it is because Armageddon is not quite what has been thought. We can note the similarity of the

descriptions of the frogs as "performers of signs" to the description of nuclear war in Chapter 13:
"He performs great signs -- startling miracles -- even making fire fall from the sky to the earth in men's sight." (v.13)
... and thereby make the connection to nuclear armaments. But how are they being used? The connection with the "dragon" relates to lies and deception and the false prophet relates to materialism and political manipulation.

Supposing the earth to be in a state of incredible turmoil due to numerous wars and now, cosmic catastrophe, the deceptive attitude of scientific materialism would be that something can be done to avert further disaster, assuming that a comet is, in fact, on a direct path toward the earth.

I believe that the description in this passage tells us that all the nations will assemble their nuclear armaments and attempt to use them to break the attraction between the earth and another cosmic body, or, deflect its path if it has not, in fact, made atmospheric contact. The implication of this passage is that the armies are gathered together to fight God in his manifestation as extra-terrestrial cosmic catastrophe, and this is reiterated in numerous other passages of scripture. And, the launching of all the warheads from the planet would serve a very beneficial purpose, assuming that nuclear war has not already occurred. It would rid the earth of these dreaded objects which would totally poison the globe if left to spill or seep after destruction by extra-terrestrial contact. Also, we must never lose sight of the fact that the actions of Satan, or the dragon, are part of the plan as explained in II Thessalonians.

Nevertheless, the effect of this effort is not clear. The result is clear, but whether it could turn out differently is not established. The result is global cataclysm:
"Then the seventh angel emptied out his bowl into the air, and a mighty voice came out of the sanctuary of heaven from the throne, saying, It is done! And there followed lightning flashes, loud rumblings, peals of thunder, and a tremendous earthquake; nothing like it has ever occurred since men dwelt on the earth, so severe and far reaching was that earthquake. The mighty city (a usage which indicates the nation) was broken into three parts, and the cities of the nations fell. And God kept in mind mighty Babylon, to make her drain the cup of His furious wrath and indignation. And every island fled and no mountains could be found. And great hailstones, as heavy as a talent (between fifty and sixty pounds), of immense size, fell from the sky on the people, and men blasphemed God for the plague of the hail, so very great was the torture of the plague." (Rev. 16, ex)

This event is echoed in Rev. 18:21:
"Then a single powerful angel took up a boulder like a great millstone and flung it into the sea, crying,

with such violence shall Babylon the great city be hurled down to destruction and shall never again be found!"

And again:

"Then I saw a single angel stationed in the sun's light, and with a mighty voice he shouted to all the birds that fly across the sky, come gather yourselves together for the Great Supper of God, that you may feast on the flesh of rulers, the flesh of generals and captains, the flesh of powerful and mighty men, the flesh of horses and their riders, and the flesh of all humanity, both small and great! Then I saw the beast and the rulers and leaders of the earth with their troops mustered to go into battle and make war against Him Who is mounted on the horse (a celestial event) and against his troops. And the beast was seized and overpowered, and with him the false prophet who in his presence had worked wonders and performed miracles by which he led astray those who had accepted or permitted to be placed upon them the stamp of the beast, and those who paid homage and gave divine honors to his image. Both of the two were hurled alive into the fiery lake that burns and blazes with brimstone." (Rev. 19, ex.)

Each of these passages is about the same event; each adding layers of color and detail. If we recall that angels were used to symbolize the planets in Jewish traditions, and considering all the related references to comets and other prophesied extra-terrestrial destruction, particularly that found in the writings of Nostradamus, I think that it is reasonable to assume that these passages describe just such an event. The common elements of all the prophetic excerpts I have compared and analyzed in this thesis are:

1.Wars, and rumors of wars, pestilence, famine.

2.Visible changes in the appearance of the sun and other horrifying signs and events in the heavens.

3.Rains of fire and meteorites.

4.Global earthquake.

5.Destruction of nearly the entire human race, particularly those inhabiting the geographic area of the "Beast"

All of these, taken together, point to one event -- the contact between the earth and another celestial body or bodies. Releasing of macrocosmic quantum potentials leading to Metamorphosis of Planet Earth and all upon it.

In the prophecies of Revelation it seems that we have been given the darkest and grimmest scenario imaginable. Is it possible for such a thing to have been foreseen over 2000 years ago? Why is that so many more recent "prophets" only talk about "positive" things? Is it because they are lying or is there is some sort of veil that prevents any

comments of a negative nature whatsoever which might act to influence the thinking of mankind?
So, what about probability? How does that figure in here?

Conclusions made from all knowledge we receive must still remain the individual choice and I think this is part of the reason that much true psychic information is delivered in somewhat ambiguous terms. The quantum probabilities have not congealed and will not congeal until the exact moment of occurrence of any event. And, to a certain extent, we can alter that right up to the last minute.

This does not mean that we cannot know -- it is just that the Universe leaves itself as many possibilities as it can. And, in larger concepts, the probabilities are end-points of directions taken long ago -- over which we have little or no control.

We have discussed the idea that prophecy is the ability to see the All and to see the probable direction we are heading. In this sense, I feel that, at the present time we are facing a quantum change which is inexorable in terms of accomplishment, but variable in terms of specifics. It will be cataclysmic -- there will be extra-terrestrial interactions -- but the severity and the timing are still in the realm of probabilities. It would take tremendous interaction on the part of every human being presently on the planet to change this destiny. In fact, I think that the only kind of change which could be manifested at this point is a spiritual elevation which would make material cataclysm an irrelevant issue.

So, it is in this sense that we need to take a look at the last, significant aspect of our world: The False Prophet. Gurdjieff recounts an important fable, recorded by Ouspensky in his book, In Search of the Miraculous:
"There is an Eastern tale which speaks about a very rich magician who had a great many sheep. But at the same time this magician was very mean. He did not want to hire shepherds, nor did he want to erect a fence about the pasture where his sheep were grazing. The sheep consequently often wandered into the forest, fell into ravines, and so on, and above all they ran away, for they knew that the magician wanted their flesh and skins and this they did not like.

"At last the magician found a remedy. He hypnotized his sheep and suggested to them first of all that they were immortal and that no harm was being done to them when they were skinned, that, on the contrary, it would be very good for them and even pleasant; secondly he suggested that the magician was a good master who loved his flock so much that he was ready to do anything in the world for them; and in the third place he suggested to them that if anything at all were going to happen to them it was not going to happen just then, at any rate not that day, and therefore they had no need to think about it. Further the magician suggested to his sheep that they were not sheep at all; to some of them he suggested that they were lions, to others that they were eagles, to others that they were men, and to others that they were magicians.

"And after this all his cares and worries about the sheep came to an end. They never ran away again but quietly awaited the time when the magician would require their flesh and skins." [Ouspensky] This accurately describes the condition of the great masses of humanity at the present time.

"In order to awaken, first of all one must realize that one is in a state of sleep. And, in order to realize that one is, indeed, in a state of sleep, one must recognize and fully understand the nature of the forces which operate to keep one in the state of sleep, or hypnosis. It is absurd to think that this can be done by seeking information from the very source which induces the hypnosis."

"Theoretically, (a man can awaken), but practically it is almost impossible because as soon as a man awakens for a moment and opens his eyes, all the forces that caused him to fall asleep begin to act upon him with tenfold energy and he immediately falls asleep again, very often dreaming that he is awake or awakening." [Ouspensky]

It is in the awakening of mankind that the hope of mitigating the prophesied disasters lies. In order to bring a halt to the conditions which have operated to bring humanity to the present deplorable conditions, they must be exposed and understood.

The False Prophet -- the strong delusion to error -- must be overcome.

"Beware of false prophets who come to you dressed as sheep but inside they are devouring wolves. You will fully recognize them by their fruits. Do people pick grapes from thorns or figs from thistles?... A good tree cannot bear bad fruit; nor can a bad tree bear excellent fruit." (Matt. 7:15,23)

While everyone will readily admit that there is probably too much violence on television and that the ads are probably pure balderdash, very few people have a real conception of the precise nature and extent of the hypnotic influence of the media. Still fewer have any idea of the purposes behind this inducement. Wallace and Wallechinsky write in The People's Almanac:

"After World War II, television flourished... Psychologists and sociologists were brought in to study human nature in relation to selling; in other words, to figure out how to manipulate people without their feeling manipulated. Dr. Ernest Dichter, President of the Institute for Motivational Research made a statement in 1941... 'the successful ad agency manipulates human motivations and desires and develops a need for goods with which the public has at one time been unfamiliar -- perhaps even undesirous of purchasing.

"Discussing the influence of television, Daniel Boorstin wrote: 'Here at last is a supermarket of surrogate experience. Successful programming offers entertainment -- under the guise of instruction; instruction -- under the guise of entertainment; political persuasion -- with the appeal of advertising; and advertising -- with the appeal of drama.'

"Programed television serves not only to spread acquiescence and conformity, but it represents a deliberate industry approach." [quoted by Wallace, Wallechinsky]

Aside from the fact that television has been conjectured to be extremely detrimental to children and that it is now thought that most of the deteriorating aspects of society can be attributed to the decaying values portrayed on television, there is a deeper and more insidious effect upon the human psyche. As quoted, it is a planned and deliberate manipulation to spread acquiescence and conformity and to hypnotize the masses to submit to the authority of the television.

Allen Funt, host of a popular show, Candid Camera, was once asked what was the most disturbing thing he had learned about people in his years of dealing

with them through the media. His response was chilling in its ramifications:
"The worst thing, and I see it over and over, is how easily people can be led by any kind of authority figure, or even the most minimal kinds of authority. A well dressed man walks up the down escalator and most people will turn around and try desperately to go up also... We put up a sign on the road, 'Delaware Closed Today'. Motorists didn't even question it. Instead they asked: 'Is Jersey open?'" [quoted by Wallace, Wallechinsky]

A picture is forming of a deliberately contrived society of televised conformity, literate and creative inadequacy, and social unrest and decadence. It is apparent that the media is in charge of propagating these conditions.

It would seem that the motivation masters would, in the interests of their industrial clients, plan programming to bring about beneficial societal conditions -- which they could, in fact, do. It is apparent that the final authority on televised programming is in the hands of the advertisers, backed by the industries whose products are being sold. With all the psychological input to which they have access, it would seem that they would force programming to correct societal conditions which cost them money. Over 25 billion dollars a year is spent to teach workers to read and write, after graduating from the combined effects of a public school system and the television. It is accepted that the burgeoning crime rate, which also costs these industrial giants vast sums of money, is mostly attributable to the frustrations and dissatisfactions engendered by the false view of reality presented over the television. Why don't they use their financial resources to back the motivation masters to figure out how to present programming which could effect positive changes? Can it be that the conditions of society, including the programed response to "minimal signs of authority" are planned? Would anyone care to suggest that the figures and studies relating to the detrimental influence of programming is not available to them and that they don't realize that it is costing them money? If that is the case, then they are too stupid to be arbiters of our values and we should disregard them entirely in any event. If it is not the case, then we must assume that there is an object to this manipulation.

There is much evidence to support the idea that this purpose, or the object of this manipulation, is to create psychological and social disunity sufficient to permit the instituting of a totalitarian government at the behest of the people. It is further theorized that the "wealthy elite" seek to control the entire world from behind the scenes and it is to this end that they mastermind and fund the various actions which appear to the masses as political and international "accidents".

FDR. said:
"Nothing in politics ever happens by accident; if it happens, you can bet it was planned!"

And he was in a position to know.

There is much evidence to support the notion that wars are fomented and fought to redistribute these balances of financial power behind the scenes and that, though our fathers, brother, grandfathers, uncles, cousins and sons die in these actions, they are merely games of "International Relations" played by those whose money and position give them little else with which to occupy their time or intelligence.

There is, however, a consequence to this game of global chess which is apparent to neither the players nor the pawns of the game.

An understanding of quantum physics makes it comprehensible that the electrical current which manifests through organic life on earth, increased by great emotional responses such as anger or hatred, or judgment could appreciably alter the flow and placement of sub-atomic particles. Multiply this by the billions of people on the planet, and you have a very great Contact Potential Difference. Add to this the deliberate manipulation of the atomic structure of the earth through nuclear testing activities, the affect is increased exponentially. The consequence is the establishment of a massive state of electrical usage. The continuing deterioration of human relations across the globe increases this Contact Potential Difference in two ways: On an individual basis through improperly controlled and inadequately developed brain wave functions; on a global basis through the use of nuclear energy either in tests, power plants or actual military actions. There is also another way we must consider.

The level and types of energy created by the societal conditions that exist today are of such a nature that at the point in time when the sun expresses its atomic nature in its regular and periodic pulsation, the conditions will be ripe for the inflow of a vast surge of electromagnetic energy far beyond our ability to comprehend or measure. In other words, organic life on Earth is the circuitry, and the bodies of the solar system are the parts of the machine.

In like manner did the former "Dyings" occur, and deterioration of atomic particles increased or accelerated so that the fossil record shows this event to have been in the past millions of years rather than the actual thousands of years. In those times, similar societal conditions created the Contact Potential Difference, but we have something NOW they didn't have -- nuclear weapons and five billion people. And, so, it is prophesied that this will be the worst cataclysm the earth has ever known.

"For just as the lightning flashes from the East and shines and is seen as far as the West so will the coming of the Son of Man be. Wherever there is a fallen body there the vultures will flock together." (Matt. 24:27,28)

"Then I saw a single angel stationed in the sun's light, and with a mighty voice he shouted to all the birds that fly across the sky come gather yourselves together for the Great Supper of God that you may feast on the flesh of rulers, the flesh of generals and captains, the flesh of powerful and mighty men, the flesh of horses and their riders and the flesh of all humanity, both free and slave, both small and great." (Revelation 19:17,18)

And here we have the hidden purpose, The Mystery of God -- the utilization of the energy potentials accumulated in organic life on earth to effect a macrocosmic quantum jump; the feeding of the cosmos by the destruction of life on earth -- The Marriage Supper of the Lamb - The creation of a New Universe via Quantum Metamorphosis.

"By faith we understand that the worlds were framed by the word of God, so that what we see was not made out of things which are visible... By faith Noah, being forewarned of God concerning events of which as yet there was no visible sign, took heed and diligently and reverently constructed and prepared an ark for the deliverance of his own family. By this faith he passed judgment and sentence on the world's unbelief and became an heir and possessor of righteousness." (Paul to the Hebrews, Chapter 11, excerpts.)

666: The Mark of the Beast

What is it?
Many Christians believe the 666 mark will be a biochip implant to create the cashless society.

Revelation 13.

Why is it so bad?

All who take the mark will be damned by God to be cast into the Lake of Fire.

Why will those who take the mark be damned?

I think it's because God made Silver and Gold as honest weights and measures to be used as money!

Money is NOT paper (which is a promise), not electronic credits, not chips, not a mark, nor a number!

The Use of Paper Money Violates All of the Ten Commandments

For more on the nature of gold and silver and why they are real money, please read my other site, silverstockreport.com

Here are the main verses on 666, the mark of the beast:

Revelation 13:16 And he causeth all, both small and great, rich and poor, free and bond, to receive a mark in their right hand, or in their foreheads:

Revelation 13:17 And that no man might buy or sell, save he that had the mark, or the name of the beast, or the number of his name.

Revelation 13:18 Here is wisdom. Let him that hath understanding count the number of the beast: for it is the number of a man; and his number is Six hundred threescore and six. (666)

Using the extended meanings of the original Greek text, Michael E. O'Brien of highpraise.com (now a dead link) created an alternate possible translation given of Rev. 13, that indicates a biochip implant containing a number like the social security number could fulfill the prophecy very precisely: Rev 13: [16] He [the second beast] caused everyone, small and great, rich and poor, free and slave, to receive an etching of servitude (made with a sharp point) in their right hand, or in their foreheads; [17] so that no one could buy or sell unless they had the etching of servitude, or the authority of the beast, or the number of his authority. [18] Here is wisdom. Let him that has understanding count the pebbles as the number of the beast, for it is an individual's [identification] number. His number is incised with a pricking action - willingly - by one claiming to possess the Godhead...

In the USA, 98-99% of all transactions are already cashless, and cash represents about 1-4% of bank deposits. (See my article, "Major Frauds of the U.S. Monetary System". Smart cards and biochip pet implants are in wide use in Europe. Many Christians strongly suspect that this "mark of the beast" prophesy will be implemented by technology that exists today, the biochip implant (syringe implantable microchip/lithium transponder), or an invisible tatoo designed to go in the right hand or forehead.

So, when will the mark of the beast come?

The technology exists today, and people are getting chips implanted under their skin today.

We have the social security number today, we have paper money today.

But I believe the final and ultimate fulfillment of the prophecy of the mark of the beast will take place in the second half of the 7 year tribulation, and before that, Christians may escape that time of trouble in the rapture.

Bibleprophesy.org -- teaching the pretribulation rapture, that I believe will come before the time of the mark of the beast.

Here are more scriptures in Revelation that talk about the mark of the beast. Note, in Revelation 19:20, the people who take the mark are deceived! This means they are tricked, or that they do not know the full implications of what they are doing. The may not realize that taking the mark is an act of worship, or that it is an evil action that God hates.

Revelation 14:9 And the third angel followed them, saying with a loud voice, If any man worship the beast and his image, and receive his mark in his forehead, or in his hand,

Revelation 14:10 The same shall drink of the wine of the wrath of God, which is poured out without mixture into the cup of his indignation; and he shall be tormented with fire and brimstone in the presence of the holy angels, and in the presence of the Lamb:

Revelation 14:11 And the smoke of their torment ascendeth up for ever and ever: and they have no rest day nor night, who worship the beast and his image, and whosoever receiveth the mark of his name.

Revelation 14:12 Here is the patience of the saints: here are they that keep the commandments of God, and the faith of Jesus.

Revelation 15:2 And I saw as it were a sea of glass mingled with fire: and them that had gotten the victory over the beast, and over his image, and over his mark, and over the number of his name, stand on the sea of glass, having the harps of God.

Revelation 16:2 And the first went, and poured out his vial upon the earth; and there fell a noisome and grievous sore upon the men which had the mark of the beast, and upon them which worshipped his image.

Revelation 19:20 And the beast was taken, and with him the false prophet that wrought miracles before him, with which he deceived them that had received the mark of the beast, and them that worshipped his image. These both were cast alive into a lake of fire burning with brimstone.

Revelation 20:4 And I saw thrones, and they sat upon them, and judgment was given unto them: and I saw the souls of them that were beheaded for the witness of Jesus, and for the word of God, and which had not worshipped the beast, neither his image, neither had received his mark upon their foreheads, or in their hands; and they lived and reigned with Christ a thousand years.

Revelation 20:5 But the rest of the dead lived not again until the thousand years were finished. This is the first resurrection.

Revelation 20:6 Blessed and holy is he that hath part in the first resurrection: on such the second death hath no power, but they shall be priests of God and of Christ, and shall reign with him a thousand years.

The move to a cashless system is not a war against cash. It is really a war against gold and silver. Paper money cash has already served it's useful purpose, to get people to forget that gold and silver are money. Cash and bonds are used to take the gold and silver away from the people.

In sum here are my prophetic views: I believe the rapture will happen before the seven year tribulation. I believe the mark of the beast will start half way through the seven year tribulation, when the Antichrist sits in the temple in Jerusalem, and demands to be worshipped as God. I believe the war of Ezekiel 38 takes place at the start of the tribulation, which will look like Armageddon. Israel is wealthy in gold and silver and cattle, and is at peace, before this war. I believe that in order for the prophecy of Ezekiel 38 to take place, the world will have to return to a world gold standard, and I believe it is likely that there will be a world government, perhaps for an entire generation before the rapture. I believe that the Great Harlot of Revelation 17-18 is the international bankers, or perhaps a few hundred familes of Jerusalem, who were prophesied to lend to the nations which helps them rule over them. The harlot is destroyed by the seventh beast which is a world kingdom with ten kings, and they give their power to the eighth beast, the Antichrist, who installs his mark of the beast economic system. His system will be against gold and silver, and he will likely use biochipping technology to implement the mark of the beast. But the mark is also a number. And remember, those who take it are supporting and worshipping the beast (governmental) system of fraudulent weights and measures instead of God's system of honest measures, such as gold and silver.

Chaos In A Major Christian Denomination Regarding Obama!

My name is Mel Sanger, an international political researcher. In February 2008 I and my group of 5 political research analysts were asked by a Major American Christian Church (can't name it for obvious reasons) to investigate whether Barack Obama had any involvement with the freemason conspiracy new world order.

The Christian organization had received numerous calls and emails from its congregational members during 2007 and early 2008 asking whether Barack Obama was the Biblical Antichrist. It would seem that there were a number of teachers in the organization who were teaching this view which was conflicting with the organizations overall general major public support for Obama.

The confusion was causing major issues inside the church and they wanted a political research team without any ties to the organization or political biases to address the matter and report back on the findings. So we gladly accepted the task of tackling this subject.

I Was Put Off By the Typical Sensationalist Views At Every Election!

Up until then I had personally dismissed criticism of Barack Obama as simple attempts to discredit one of the most incredible political journeys not only in US history, but World History. Obama's rise was on par with the release of Nelson Mandela and the Freedom speech of Martin Luther King decades ago.

I had been re-energized by his speeches and his story. I had read his biography "Dreams of My Father" and had personally bought 10 of his biographies for a local community, for them to loan out to deprived young people who needed proof that they could succeed against the odds.

My negativity to criticism on Obama (especially those saying he was the Antichrist) had largely been because of the shoddy sensationalist things written about him, especially on YouTube.

For instance, on YouTube there were many video's linking Barack Obama's name to 666 conspiracies. Others had provided pictures of Obama not saluting the American Flag. Under full research analysis, most, if not all of these accusations were simply poor primary evidence and shoddy outstretched research with absolutely no credibility.

5000 Hours of Painstaking Analysis!

Between March 2008 and September 2008 our research group examined over 4000 pieces of documentation and conspiracy theories regarding the coming New World Order and the key people involved, both those in the public spotlight and others who remain behind the scenes.

The purpose of the research was to see identify substantial links to Barack Obama or any of the key people associated with him, and to understand his political ideology, views on faith and morals and religious associations.

We studied more than 5000 hours worth of footage on all his speeches, looking out for views, comments or words which may carry coded or cryptic messages missed by the general public but discerned by others.

A New Sickening Discovery!

In June 2008 after assessing over 3000 pieces of documentation our research team uncovered some damning and frightening evidence that completely changed our view of him Totally.

The information was so startling that at first we refused to believe it but additional analysis of confidential documents made our fears come true and it was an undeniable fact. There was a sickening feeling in the pit of my stomach because I literally had to undo everything I had liked about this man in light of the chilling evidence.

In September 2008 we published the findings in a report called the Antichrist Identity. The title is slightly misleading as we do not believe that he is the biblical Antichrist. However there is iron clad research and evidence that confirms that he is a major pawn in the new world order and one of the most dangerous US presidents ever to hold office.

He is also progressing the antichrist system that is is gathering pace after the recent world economic upheaval.

The report also implicates not only Barack Obama but also Javier Solana of the European Union, Prince Charles of Wales, Queen Beatrix of Netherlands and Prince Hassan of Jordan.

The report implicates a secret network of people who all know each others world roles and who are acting independently publicly, but are coercing a plan behind the public scene to use their powers of influence to take the world to a new level of world regulation.

Why Are The Christian Experts Asleep?
You would have thought that the christian community would have discerned this but unfortunately much of the christian community is asleep on this matter. Bible Prophecy Ministries who week in, week out, publish so much information about the coming new world order are silent on this specific matter.

In fact nearly all of the bible prophecy ministries we have contacted and asked to air our report all of them, 100% have refused to even respond.

Others are sitting on the fence. Clearly they can sense something weird has been triggered in the political dimension but whether its for fear of losing their airtime on TV, Radio, many simply skirt around the issue suggesting that "we need to pray for Obama" and going no further.

At a recent international bible prophecy conference, did you know that after 3 days of lectures and presentations there was absolutely nothing said about "Obama and the New World Order" or "The Masonic deception by which the New world Order will be executed".....

There was lots of talk and discussion about the rapture, the tribulation, the economic meltdown, the European Union, commitment to Israel etc but absolutely nothing about the dangers of the Obama New World Order, or why is it, that the political leadership of Israel are freemasons, or the purpose of the rebuilding Of Solomon's Temple in Jerusalem from an occultist perspective.

Skirting with the broad issues but not dealing with the detail.....Unfortunately the devil is in the detail!

The Second Coming of Jesus Christ

One only has to read a newspaper or listen to a newscast in order to see Bible prophecy being fulfilled. There have been more prophecies fulfilled in the twentieth century than in any other time in church history. We believe there is a great reason for this. We believe that the time is rapidly approaching for the Lord Jesus Christ to return to this earth and take the kingdoms of this world for Himself.

In this tract, we will attempt to show you from God's word the chronological order of future prophetic events. That is, we will attempt to TEACH you some basic Bible doctrine about the Second Coming. It is our prayer that you will read carefully through these pages, asking the Holy Spirit of God to lead and guide you through the truths in His word (John. 16:13). Please check all Scripture references very carefully for a better understanding. May God richly bless your study.

The Coming Righteous Kingdom

The main theme of the Bible is the Lord Jesus Christ, and the main subject is the Kingdom that His Father has promised Him. There are many Bible prophecies that speak of this coming King and Kingdom. Some are as follows:

"The sceptre shall not depart from Judah, nor a lawgiver from between his feet, until Shiloh come; and unto him shall the gathering of the people be." (Gen. 49:10)

"Why do the heathen rage, and the people imagine a vain thing? The kings of the earth set themselves, and the rulers take counsel together, against the LORD, and against his anointed, saying, Let us break their bands asunder, and cast away their cords from us. He that sitteth in the heavens shall laugh: the Lord shall have them in derision. Then shall he speak unto them in his wrath, and vex them in his sore displeasure. Yet have I set my king upon my holy hill of Zion. I will declare the decree: the LORD hath said unto me, Thou art my Son; this day have I begotten thee. Ask of me, and I shall give thee the heathen for thine inheritance, and the uttermost parts of the earth for thy possession." (Psa. 2:1-8)

"And there shall come forth a rod out of the stem of Jesse, and a Branch shall grow out of his roots: And the spirit of the LORD shall rest upon him, the spirit of wisdom and understanding, the spirit of counsel and might, the spirit of knowledge and of the fear of the LORD; And shall make him of quick understanding in the fear of the LORD: and he shall not judge after the sight of his eyes, neither reprove after the hearing of his ears: But with righteousness shall he judge the poor, and reprove with equity for the meek of the earth: and he shall smite the earth with the rod of his mouth, and with the breath of his lips shall he slay the wicked. And righteousness shall be the girdle of his loins, and faithfulness the girdle of his reins. The wolf also shall dwell with the lamb, and the leopard shall lie down with the kid; and the calf and the young lion and the fatling together; and a little child shall lead them." (Isa. 11:1-6)

"Behold, the days come, saith the LORD, that I will raise unto David a righteous Branch, and a King shall reign and prosper, and shall execute judgment and justice in the earth." (Jer. 23:5)

Such Old Testament verses as these state very clearly that God intends to set the Lord Jesus Christ up as King over the earth. There have been many kings to rise and fall throughout history, but God has in mind a PERFECT King for His promised Kingdom.

Coming to the New Testament we find that God still has this Kingdom very much in mind. In Luke chapter one, verses thirty-one through thirty-three, the angel says to Mary:

"And, behold, thou shalt conceive in thy womb, and bring forth a son, and shalt call his name JESUS. He shall be great, and shall be called the Son of the Highest: and the Lord God shall give unto him the throne of his father David: And he shall reign over the house of Jacob for ever; and of his kingdom there shall be no end."

John the Baptist came preaching that this Kingdom was at hand in Matthew 3:2, and Jesus also preached this message when He began to preach (Mat. 4:17).

During the actual ministry of Christ, He preached mostly to His people, the Jews (Mat. 10:5-6; 15:24), because Israel is the one nation that God chose long ago to be a shining light to this lost and dying world. In Isaiah 62:1 God says, "For Zion's sake will I not hold my peace, and for Jerusalem's sake I will not rest, until the righteousness thereof go forth as brightness, and the salvation thereof as a lamp that burneth." God will not rest until His chosen nation is established in the earth as a BURNING LAMP (Gen. 15:17) to this lost and dying world. Starting with Abraham in Genesis chapter twelve, God begins to focus on ONE CHOSEN PEOPLE to bring forth His King for the coming Kingdom. All of the promises that God made to Abraham and his descendants are still in effect today, and they will soon reach their fulfillment, for the Kingdom WILL come.

Many teach that the Kingdom promises are no longer valid, because the Jews rejected Christ, but this is a false teaching. In Acts 1:6-7, before Jesus ascended into Heaven, the apostles asked Him about this Kingdom, saying, " . . . Lord, wilt thou at this time restore again the kingdom to Israel?" If the Kingdom promises were no longer valid, then Jesus would have told them so, but instead He says, "...It is not for you to know the times or the seasons, which the Father hath put in his own power." So Israel's rejection of Christ doesn't make void the promises of God. God will chastise the Jews for their sin, and then He will restore the Kingdom to Israel (Psa. 89:29-36).

Someone says, "If the Jews won't receive their King, then how can God restore the Kingdom? Doesn't this put God in some sort of a jam?" No, God has a master plan. He knows exactly what He will do. In Hebrews 8:8-10, we read some interesting words quoted from Jeremiah chapter 31: "For finding fault with them, he saith, Behold, the days come, saith the Lord, when I will make a new covenant with the house of Israel and with the house of Judah: Not according to the covenant that I made with their fathers in the day when I took them by the hand to lead them out of the land of Egypt; because they continued not in my covenant, and I regarded them not, saith the Lord. For this is the covenant that I will make with the house of Israel after those days, saith the Lord; I will put my laws into their mind, and write them in their hearts: and I will be to them a God, and they shall be to me a people:"

The words "after those days" clearly refer to a future time when Israel will be converted to the Lord Jesus Christ. Paul tells us in Romans 11:25-27 that Israel has been BLINDED for this present age, but that "all Israel shall be saved" because God will "take away their sins." God promised Israel a Kingdom, so there WILL be a Kingdom.

Since this Kingdom wasn't established at the First Coming of Christ, it must be established at the Second Coming. God knew that the Jews would reject His Son; so He predetermined that Christ's shed Blood on Calvary would serve as an atonement for the sin of the world. This was God's plan all along--to come into the world and pay for the sins of all men (Jhn. 1:29; Rev. 13:8). So the First Coming was one of suffering and shame, but the Second Coming will be one of glory, honor, and praise (1 Pet. 1:10-12). The first time Jesus received a crown of thorns, but when He comes again He will have MANY crowns (Rev. 19:12). He was the "lamb of God" when He came the first time, but He will be the "lion of the tribe of Judah" the second time (Rev. 5:5). The First Coming gave Jesus Christ to the world, but the Second Coming will give the world to Jesus Christ! Just as David was chosen to be the king of Israel many years before he actually received the kingdom (1 Sam. 16), the Lord Jesus Christ has been chosen to take over the kingdoms of this world and rule as God's "KING OF KINGS" (Rev. 11:15; 19:16).

A "Christianity" without a Second Coming is a very selfish religion, for it robs Jesus Christ of all God's precious promises to Him. The teaching and preaching of the Second Coming is very essential, because it speaks of God's righteous King returning to this earth and taking what rightfully belongs to Him. Christians should be rejoicing! The Lord Jesus Christ, the Captain of your Salvation (if you're saved), will soon return to this earth and set things in order and YOU can be on the winning side!

The Pre-Millennial View

The first few verses of Revelation chapter twenty speak of this coming Kingdom being one thousand years long. Verse six says that the saints will reign with Christ for a thousand years. That is, we will reign with Him for a thousand literal years in a literal, physical, and visible earthly Kingdom, and then we will reign forever in the New Heavens and the New Earth (Rev. 5:10; 22:5; 11:15; chapters 21 and 22).

Many these days are teaching false doctrines about the Millennium (the one thousand-year reign). Some teach the "Post-Millennial" view, believing that mankind will become good enough to usher in this righteous Kingdom WITHOUT Jesus Christ. Post-Millennialism teaches that the Church's influence on the world will become stronger and stronger, and the world will become better and better until we all enter a happy golden age of peace and prosperity. At the end of this utopian age, the Lord Jesus Christ will supposedly return and reward the Church for a job well done.

A more popular view is the "A-millennial" view. This is the false teaching that there will be no Millennium, only a "general judgment" someday and that's all.

Both of the above views are heresy, for the Bible teaches that there WILL be a Millennium, and it teaches that it will not begin until the Lord Jesus Christ returns and establishes it and rules over it Himself. This means that only the "PRE-MILLENNIAL" view is correct. This is the doctrine that Christ will return BEFORE the Millennium to destroy the wicked, take over the kingdoms of this world, and set up the Kingdom that His Father has promised Him. Pre-Millennialism correctly says that there will be no world peace until the Prince of Peace returns (Isa. 9:6). Pre-Millennialism has a very NEGATIVE outlook toward this present world system, as does the Bible, but a very POSITIVE outlook toward the soon appearing of the King of Kings. A Christian who holds the Pre-Millennial view is a Christian who believes exactly what God says about giving His beloved Son the kingdoms of this world.

Now, before the Millennium can begin, there are many prophecies that must be fulfilled. These prophecies must be RIGHTLY DIVIDED (2 Tim. 2:15) or confusion and heresy will prevail. We must study Bible prophecy SCRIPTURE with SCRIPTURE, allowing the Holy Spirit to guide us into all truth (John. 16:13). Now let's look at some more significant events in Bible prophecy.

The Restoration of Israel

God cannot establish His Son in Israel as King of the Jews unless the Jews are living in Palestine, their promised homeland, so it is God's plan to restore the Jews to Palestine before the Second Coming of Christ:

"But, The LORD liveth, that brought up the children of Israel from the land of the north, and from all the lands whither he had driven them: and I will bring them again into their land that I gave unto their fathers." (Jer. 16:15)

"And I will bring again the captivity of my people of Israel, and they shall build the waste cities, and inhabit them; and they shall plant vineyards, and drink the wine thereof; they shall also make gardens, and eat the fruit of them. And I will plant them upon their land, and they shall no more be pulled up out of their land which I have given them, saith the LORD thy God." (Amos 9:14-15)

Because Israel rejected Christ, God allowed the Romans to destroy Jerusalem in 70 A.D., and the Jews were dispersed among the Gentile nations of the world. Since then they have wondered from nation to nation suffering bitter persecution. However, in the late 1800's a remarkable thing started happening. In large numbers, the Jews began returning to Palestine, and in 1887 they made formal statements that they intended to REPOSSESS THEIR HOMELAND!

When World War I began in 1914, there were 80,000 Jews living in Palestine. England's Balfour Declaration of 1917 gave strong approval for the Jews to establish a national homeland, but England reneged due to Arab pressure. Nevertheless, 400,000 Jews had settled in the homeland by 1939. Satan saw what was happening. He knew that the Lord was regathering the Jews for a reason, and he knew the reason: the Second Coming of Christ. So Satan raised up Adolph Hitler to murder six million of God's chosen people as an outright act of hate and revenge. This massive slaughter created enough sympathy for the Jews that the United Nations granted 5000 square miles of Palestinian land to them after World War II. Then in 1948 Israel became an independent nation for the first time in many centuries! The Arabs have fought viciously to destroy Israel, but with no success. God wants His people IN PALESTINE (Amos 9:14-15), because the Lord Jesus Christ is coming very soon. During the Six Day War of 1967, Israel even gained possession of the ancient temple sight, and plans are currently underway to rebuild the temple.

Jesus likens Israel unto a "fig tree" in Matthew 24:32-34, and He likens the restoration of Israel unto a fig tree putting forth leaves. He said that He would return during the same generation which witnesses Israel putting forth leaves as a nation. We are living in that generation! There are some four million Jews living in Palestine today. We have seen the Jews return to Palestine, and we have seen the nation of Israel prosper. Friend, there's a reason for all of this: the Lord Jesus Christ is coming soon!

The Rapture of the Church
Up until now, we've said very little about the Church, because Bible prophecy deals mainly with Israel, but the Church is also very important. In fact, the Church has a very SPECIAL relationship with Christ: she is His BRIDE (Eph. 5:25-32; Rev. 19:7-9).

Before God can swing His full attention back to Israel, He must fulfill certain promises that He has made to the Church. While He has spent the last two thousand years chastising Israel for her disobedience, He has also been calling out a Gentile bride for the Lord Jesus Christ. Just as

Joseph found a Gentile bride while he was separated from his brethren (Gen. 41:45), Jesus finds a Gentile bride while He is separated from the Jews. It is true that many Jews have been saved by receiving Christ, but most have not. The Church consists mostly of converted Gentiles. God is taking out from among the Gentiles a people for His name, and then He will once again take up His dealings with Israel as a nation. Notice what the Bible says in Acts 15:14-16:

"Simeon hath declared how God at the first did visit the Gentiles, to take out of them a people for his name. And to this agree the words of the prophets; as it is written, After this I will return, and will build again the tabernacle of David, which is fallen down; and I will build again the ruins thereof, and I will set it up:"

In the near future God will put Israel through a very troublesome period of time known as the "great tribulation" (Mat. 24:21), but Christians will not have to endure the Tribulation. Paul tells us in 1 Thessalonians 1:10 that the Church is waiting for the Lord from Heaven, not for the Great Tribulation, because He has delivered us from the wrath to come. 1 Thessalonians 5:9 says that God has not appointed us (Christians) to wrath, but to obtain salvation through Christ. Those who have been "born again" (John 3:3) will soon be "caught up" to Heaven without dying. Notice what the word of God says:

"Behold, I show you a mystery; We shall not all sleep, but we shall all be changed, In a moment, in the twinkling of an eye, at the last trump: for the trumpet shall sound, and the dead shall be raised incorruptible, and we shall be changed." (1 Cor. 15:51-52)

"For the Lord himself shall descend from heaven with a shout, with the voice of the archangel, and with the trump of God: and the dead in Christ shall rise first: Then we which are alive and remain shall be caught up together with them in the clouds, to meet the Lord in the air: and so shall we ever be with the Lord. Wherefore comfort one another with these words." (1 Ths. 4:16-18)

It is a "comfort" for Christians to have this blessed promise. It would NOT be a comfort if Christians had to endure the Great Tribulation. Our merciful Lord will call the Church out of this world BEFORE the Tribulation starts. After all, the Church was never really a part of this evil world system anyhow (Jas. 4:4; Rom. 12:2; Col. 3:2)! We're just passing through this world to a much better place (Gal. 4:26), and we will be leaving very soon! What about you?

This great departure of the saints is pictured on various occasions in the Bible. Just as God took Enoch out of the world before the flood (Gen. 5:24; Heb. 11:5), He will take His Church out of the world before the Tribulation. Just as God delivered Lot and his family from the violent judgment upon Sodom (Gen. 19:22-24), He will deliver His saints from the coming judgment of the Great Tribulation. Like any responsible Father, God will take proper care of His children. He will destroy the Devil's children (Jhn. 8:44; 1 Jhn. 3:10), but His own children are safe and secure. As Psalm 145:20 assures us, "The LORD preserveth all them that love him: but all the wicked will he destroy."

This calling-out of the Church is commonly referred to as the "Rapture" because of the quick and surprising nature in which it occurs. The world will stand in shock when millions of Christians suddenly vanish from the face of the earth! The freeways, the subways, the airports and streets will be in a total shambles as thousands and thousands of drivers suddenly vanish from their seats! No doubt, millions of people will be killed immediately.

Those remaining alive will be in shock as they search for their loved ones among all the demolished cars and buildings. Communications will also be greatly disrupted, because many key communications people will be caught up in the Rapture.

Opportunists will add to the confusion by looting and killing. They'll feel that during such an emergency they can get away with anything. There will be worldwide chaos!

Authorities may attempt to explain the millions of missing people, but make no mistake about it: GOD TOOK THEM! He promised that He would call out His people, so He will call them out. That's all there is to it.

Many people laugh and make jokes about this Bible doctrine, but there's coming a day when the laughing will end. Noah was a preacher of righteousness who probably received a great deal of mocking and ridicule from the world as he built the ark upon dry ground, but the mocking stopped when the flood waters began to rise. God was true to His word then, and God will be true to His word today. Jesus is coming soon, and you will either be caught up to meet Him, or you will be left behind to enter the Great Tribulation. The choice is yours.

The Judgment Seat of Christ

Once Christians have been caught up to Heaven, we will appear before the Judgment Seat of Christ to be judged by the Lord for our Christian service. Paul wrote about this judgment to the Romans and to the Corinthians:

"But why dost thou judge thy brother? or why dost thou set at nought thy brother? for we shall all stand before the judgment seat of Christ." (Rom. 14:10)

"For other foundation can no man lay than that is laid, which is Jesus Christ. Now if any man build upon this foundation gold, silver, precious stones, wood, hay, stubble; Every man's work shall be made manifest: for the day shall declare it, because it shall be revealed by fire; and the fire shall try every man's work of what sort it is. If any man's work abide which he hath built thereupon, he shall receive a reward. If any man's work shall be burned, he shall suffer loss: but he himself shall be saved; yet so as by fire." (1 Cor. 3:11-15)

"For we must all appear before the judgment seat of Christ; that every one may receive the things done in his body, according to that he hath done, whether it be good or bad." (2 Cor. 5:10)

As these verses reveal, a Christian isn't judged to determine his eternal destiny. A Christian's eternal destiny is established the moment he receives Jesus Christ as Savior. The Judgment Seat of Christ is for judging the Christian's SERVICE while on this earth. Rewards will be given to some, while others will lose rewards (2 Jhn. 8), but no one goes to Hell at this judgment.

After the Judgment Seat of Christ, we (Christians) will wait with the Lord in Heaven until the Great Tribulation is over on earth. We will then take part in the Marriage of the Lamb and in the Marriage Supper of the Lamb (Rev. 19:7-9). This is when the Lord Jesus Christ and His Bride, the Church, are officially united.

We will then return with the Lord to the earth, and He will destroy the wicked and establish the Millennial Kingdom, and His saints will reign with Him on earth for one thousand years (Rev. 20:1-7).

The Great Tribulation

Jesus said in Matthew 24:21, "For then shall be great tribulation, such as was not since the beginning of the world to this time, no, nor ever shall be."

It will be during this short time period that the wicked Antichrist will rise to power and dictate the world. He will have nearly everyone deceived into believing that he is the answer to their many troubles (Rev. 13:3). Those who reject the truth today will fall for his lies in the Tribulation, because God will send them "strong delusion," causing them to believe a lie (2 Ths. 2:11-12). The Antichrist will have supernatural powers and great charisma. People will gladly follow after him (Rev. 13:5, 13-14; 2 Ths. 2:7-10).

All of the horrible events in Revelation chapters six through nineteen will occur during the Tribulation. In fact, most of these events will occur during a forty-two month time period, which is the last half of the Tribulation (Rev. 11:2; 13:5). There will be war, famine, and death (Rev. 6:2-8). Satan will have power to kill one fourth of the earth's population (Rev. 6:8), and many who choose to follow Christ at this time will be killed (Rev. 6:9; 20:4). There will be great earthquakes (Rev. 6:12), awesome changes in the skies (Rev. 6:13-14; 8:8, 12), and men will be tormented five months by the horrible locust creatures of Revelation chapter nine. In addition to all of this, Satan and his angels will be cast out into the earth (Rev. 12:9)!

Once Satan has been cast down to the earth, he will incarnate himself into a man and become the Antichrist. Just as Jesus was "God manifest in the flesh," Antichrist will be Satan manifest in the flesh. According to Revelation 13:16-18, this "beast" (Antichrist) will cause everyone to receive a mark in their right hand or in their forehead. This mark will allow people to buy and sell, and no one will be permitted to buy and sell without it. The number "666" will be connected with the mark, and credit cards, checks, and debit cards will become useless, while computerized scanning devices in the stores will keep track of bank account debits and credits. Everyone MUST take the Mark of the Beast, and Hell awaits those who do (Rev. 14:11). For further reading about this subject, please write for our tract titled Signs of the Times.

The Soviet Union will continue with their "democratic reform," and the European Communities will also be unified with their "United States in Europe" as they've dreamed of for so long (Rev. 17:12-13). The world will think that universal peace has been achieved. The Antichrist will head up the "New World Order" that so many are talking about today. He will even confirm a seven year peace treaty with the nation of Israel (Dan. 9:27). Everyone will think that peace and safety has arrived at last, but the Bible says, "For when they shall say, Peace and safety; then sudden destruction cometh upon them, as travail upon a woman with child; and they shall not escape." (1 Ths. 5:3) Satan, the "god of this world" is leading this world into a trap that will damn billions to Hell forever (Rev. 12:9).

In the middle of the Tribulation the Antichrist will turn against Israel (Dan. 9:27). He will enter the rebuilt temple in Jerusalem and sit down in the Holy Place and demand to be worshipped as God (2 Ths. 2:3-4). Satan desired to have Jesus worship him in Matthew 4:9, and he WILL have the world worshipping him in the Tribulation. Those who refuse will be killed (Rev. 6:9; 20:4).

However, God will preserve a faithful remnant of Jews throughout this period (Rev. 12:6; Hos. 2:14-17), because He still plans to send Jesus back to establish the promised Kingdom. The Antichrist will think that he has taken full control and that nothing can stop him. The humanists, the liberals, and the New Agers will think that they've finally won in their struggle to wipe out all traces of Bible-believing Christianity. While Satan is laughing in the face of God, thinking that he has won and that the kingdoms of this world will NEVER belong to the Lord Jesus Christ, all the hosts of Heaven will be rejoicing, because THE GREATEST SHOW ON EARTH IS JUST BEGINNING!

Christ's Second Advent

"And I saw heaven opened, and behold a white horse; and he that sat upon him was called Faithful and True, and in righteousness he doth judge and make war. His eyes were as a flame of fire, and on his head were many crowns; and he had a name written, that no man knew, but he himself. And he was clothed with a vesture dipped in blood: and his name is called The Word of God. And the armies which were in heaven followed him upon white horses, clothed in fine linen, white and clean. And out of his mouth goeth a sharp sword, that with it he should smite the nations: and he shall rule them with a rod of iron: and he treadeth the winepress of the fierceness and wrath of Almighty God. And he hath on his vesture and on his thigh a name written, KING OF KINGS, AND LORD OF LORDS. And I saw an angel standing in the sun; and he cried with a loud voice, saying to all the fowls that fly in the midst of heaven, Come and gather yourselves together unto the supper of the great God; That ye may eat the flesh of kings, and the flesh of captains, and the flesh of mighty men, and the flesh of horses, and of them that sit on them, and the flesh of all men, both free and bond, both small and great. And I saw the beast, and the kings of the earth, and their armies, gathered together to make war against him that sat on the horse, and against his army. And the beast was taken, and with him the false prophet that wrought miracles before him, with which he deceived them that had received the mark of the beast, and them that worshipped his image. These both were cast alive into a lake of fire burning with brimstone. And the remnant were slain with the sword of him that sat upon the horse, which sword proceeded out of his mouth: and all the fowls were filled with their flesh." (Rev. 19:11-21)

"Immediately after the tribulation of those days shall the sun be darkened, and the moon shall not give her light, and the stars shall fall from heaven, and the powers of the heavens shall be shaken: And then shall appear the sign of the Son of man in heaven: and then shall all the tribes of the earth mourn, and they shall see the Son of man coming in the clouds of heaven with power and great glory." (Mat. 24:29-30)
"And it shall come to pass in the last days, that the mountain of the Lord's house shall be established in the top of the mountains, and shall be exalted above the hills; and all nations shall flow unto it. And many people shall go and say, Come ye, and let us go up to the mountain of the LORD, to the house of the God of Jacob; and he will teach us of his ways, and we will walk in his paths: for out of Zion shall go forth the law, and the word of the LORD from Jerusalem. And he shall judge among the nations, and shall rebuke many people: and they shall beat their swords into plowshares, and

their spears into pruninghooks: nation shall not lift up sword against nation, neither shall they learn war any more." (Isa. 2:2-4)

"And the seventh angel sounded; and there were great voices in heaven, saying, The kingdoms of this world are become the kingdoms of our Lord, and of his Christ; and he shall reign for ever and ever." (Rev 11:15)

These are just a few of the many prophecies to be fulfilled when Jesus returns to this earth to take over the kingdoms of this world. This will be a time of JUSTICE and JUDGMENT on the earth. The Antichrist and the False Prophet will be cast into the Lake of Fire (Rev. 19:20), and Satan himself will be chained in the "bottomless pit" for the duration of the Millennial Kingdom (Rev. 20:1-7). The nations of the earth will be judged by the Lord Jesus Christ, and some will be admitted into the Kingdom, while others will not (Mat. 25:31-46; Joel. 3:1-2).

Once all wickedness has been defeated, the Lord Jesus Christ will rule over the earth in righteousness from the Throne of His Glory in Jerusalem. He will be the King of all kings, and all nations will be subject unto Him. Friend, the Kingdom will come and the King of kings will reign.

The Millennial Reign
This will be the great "golden age" which the ancient philosophers only dreamed about. This will

be GOD'S New World Order, rather than man's. This will be a time of world peace, for the Prince of Peace will be ruling the world in righteousness (Isa. 9:6; Luk. 1:32; Isa. 2:2-4).

There will be only ONE RELIGION during the Millennium. Those who refuse to worship Christ will be punished (Zec. 14:16-19).

People will be happy during this time, because Satan will no longer be around to tempt them. The curse of Genesis chapter three will be lifted, and men will once again live long lives as they did in the days of Adam, Noah, and Methuselah (Isa. 33:24; 65:20).

There will be better farming and weather conditions (Isa. 30:23-26; Amos 9:13-15; Joel 2:19-24; Ezk. 36:29-30), and wild animals will become tame (Isa. 11:6-9; Rom. 8:20-21).

The so-called "lost tribes" of Israel will be fully restored to their proper land divisions (Ezk. 36-48).

Jerusalem will be the capital city of the world (Jer. 3:17; Mic. 4:8), and the violent acts of Arab terrorism will not be tolerated. Justice will be executed in the earth like never before. Good will overcome evil. Things will be done on earth as they are in Heaven (Mat. 6:10). Christ and His saints will reign over the earth for one thousand years!

Are You Ready?

There isn't enough space in this tract to cover the reasons why we believe the Lord's return is very near. Our Signs of the Times tract covers this subject in detail, and is freely available upon request. What we would like to address in closing is your PERSONAL SALVATION. Friend, have you ever turned from your sins and received the Lord Jesus Christ as your Savior? The Bible says, "For God so loved the world, that he gave his only begotten Son, that whosoever believeth in him should not perish, but have everlasting life." (John. 3:16)

Many have the idea that our good works can save us and get us into Heaven, but the Bible says this isn't so:

"As it is written, There is none righteous, no, not one:" (Rom. 3:10)

"For all have sinned, and come short of the glory of God;" (Rom. 3:23)

"For by grace are ye saved through faith; and that not of yourselves: it is the gift of God: Not of works, lest any man should boast." (Eph. 2:8-9)

We have no really "good" works, because we're all SINNERS by nature. We were born into this world as sinners (Psa. 51:5), and this is why Jesus said we must be "born again" (Jhn. 3:3).

This new birth is given to us freely, and was made possible when Christ died and shed His blood at Calvary for our sins. By receiving Jesus Christ as your Savior, trusting Him alone to save you, you can be born again. You can have eternal life TODAY by faith in Jesus Christ. Romans 10:13 says, "For whosoever shall call upon the name of the Lord shall be saved." Romans 10:9-10 says, "That if thou shalt confess with thy mouth the Lord Jesus, and shalt believe in thine heart that God hath raised him from the dead, thou shalt be saved. For with the heart man believeth unto righteousness; and with the mouth confession is made unto salvation."

Friend, why not turn from your sins right now and call upon the Lord to save your soul? Receive Jesus Christ as your Savior and serve Him faithfully until He returns.

If you've received Christ as your Savior, then we urge you to follow the Lord in baptism, and we also advise you to find a good Bible-believing church and join it. If we can assist you in any way, please contact us. If you need more information about salvation, please write and ask for a copy of Understanding God's Salvation Plan.

May the Lord find you ready to meet Him at His coming.

Is the end near?

I hope you have been able to read this book without too many pauses. We are dealing with some very mysterious things and we might loose track of them if we pause.

However, I want you to pause to look at what (was, is, will be) happening. There are many indicators that the NWO is being pushed hard by our own government.

Take, for instance, the push to legalize all those 12 million illegals that are presently in our country. You have to get more people on their side. That would mean 12 million more votes for the Democrats.

The proposed tax on all your financial dealings. One percent tax on all deposits and withdrawals. Then you couldn't even move your own money around without paying the NWO. Doesn't sound like much until you read the long list of taxes that are already imposed on the citizens.

Planning to take away the home mortgage deduction. Now the incentive to buy a home has diminished greatly.

Secretary of State, Hillary Clinton, has recommended to BO that the US sign the UN directive that all personal guns be banned or registered. Just another means of reducing the rights of all Americans.

Some of the Taxes Americans Pay Each Year

If you don't read it all, go to the ending then you may want to. Isn't this amazing?
Accounts Receivable Tax
Building Permit Tax
Capital Gains Tax
CDL license Tax
Cigarette Tax
Corporate Income Tax
Court Fines (indirect taxes)
Dog License Tax
Federal Income Tax
Federal Unemployment Tax (FUTA)
Fishing License Tax
Food License Tax
Fuel permit tax
Gasoline Tax (42 cents per gallon)
Hunting License Tax
Inheritance Tax Interest expense (tax on the money)
Inventory tax IRS Interest Charges (tax on top of tax)
IRS Penalties (tax on top of tax)
Liquor Tax
Local Income Tax
Luxury Taxes
Marriage License Tax

Medicare Tax
Property Tax
Real Estate Tax
Septic Permit Tax
Service Charge Taxes
Social Security Tax
Road Usage Taxes (Truckers)
Sales Taxes
Recreational Vehicle Tax
Road Toll Booth Taxes
School Tax
State Income Tax
State Unemployment Tax (SUTA)
Telephone federal excise tax
Telephone federal universal service fee tax
Telephone federal, state and local surcharge taxes
Telephone minimum usage surcharge tax
Telephone recurring and non-recurring charges tax
Telephone state and local tax
Telephone usage charge tax
Toll Bridge Taxes
Toll Tunnel Taxes
Traffic Fines (indirect taxation)
Trailer registration tax
Utility Taxes
Vehicle License Registration Tax
Vehicle Sales Tax
Watercraft registration Tax
Well Permit Tax
Workers Compensation Tax
COMMENTS: Not one of these taxes existed 100 years ago and our nation was the most prosperous

in the world, had absolutely no national debt, had the largest middle class in the world and Mom stayed home to raise the kids.   What the hell happened?

Those that are making these requests or suggestions are the ones that see themselves in the "leaders" seat in the NWO. You can bet that if they were part of the "slaves" they wouldn't be recommending these things.

Also look at the money angle.   Those that are driving the NWO have more money than they know what to do with it. It's called being in the "cat bird's seat".   They can almost taste the greatness of being in "charge of the world".   They have all forgotten one thing. They are not now nor never will be in charge of the world. God has reserved that right for Himself. His only fault, in my opinion, is to have given man so much freedom to choose.

I think you can see that these mysterious things have been going on for some time. My home town has a Masonic Temple and it was always mysterious to me. I never saw anyone go in or out, but I'm sure they did. Also what they did was a big question in my mind. It was almost like a haunted mansion.

The preceding pages have shown you that very few Presidents have been free of these "secret societies".   Even though I didn't mention every president, doesn't mean that they didn't belong. Those that weren't mentioned probably had less to do with the societies than the others.

It is amazing to realize that those with "big bucks" believe that it is their duty to establish a new world order. These people also believe that there will only be two "groups" of citizens when this comes about; the leaders and the slaves. Doesn't that make you feel good? Just think, we don't have to put up with that class of people that generally made this world turn in the first place. The middle class will revert to the slave class. I'm afraid that the ruling class is already booked up.

Did you see anyone on the "member's list" that you recognized? This list doesn't include the latest entries, but you can still visualize who might be added.

Is this something that can be reversed? By reading everything you can about "The New World Order" it would seem like it already is too far along to turn around. However, if it is God's will that this happen doesn't necessarily mean it can't be turned around. God has compromised a number of times if there is a good argument to do so.

It also needs to be remembered that no one knows when the last day will come; not even Jesus. So we have to be prepared everyday.

Before I close this writing, I wish to promote one person, that I believe to be wholly worthy of taking over the reins of government and turning this nightmare around. I do not believe that she is associated with any secret society and obligated to support their agenda. She are well known and is a credit to the human race.

Sarah Palin is one of the brightest stars in the universe. I don't know who she would pick to run with her, but you can bet that it would be a good match.

Sarah Palin is the kind of person that seems to know what is best all the time and she is not afraid to do it. People may not like how she does things, but she gets them done.

It's about time we turned this bloody mess over to people that can do more than one thing at a time. The men holding the top jobs in Washington are doing a terrible job on a daily basis. They are not the "brains" they want us to believe.

If this lady accepts this task, I know that a much better result will come forth. Pray that this kind of change will happen in 2012. Our country needs the best direction we can give it.

Ron

PS - I had also picked Condoleezza Rice for a Vice President position, but re-reading my book she was listed as a member of the CFR (Council on Foreign Relations) and that is associated with the "New World Order". If she would denounce that, she would be an ideal candidate.

May God have

mercy on our souls.